D0404033

there's more to Quitting Drinking

than Quitting Drinking

Recovery can't take place without abstinence but abstinence alone is not recovery

Dr. Paul O.

For alcoholics and other addicted individuals in recovery

SABRINA PUBLISHING
Laguna Niguel, CA
1995

SABRINA PUBLISHING
P.O. Box 6722
Laguna Niguel, CA 92607-6722

Printed in the United States of America
Front cover and supervision of design and printing by Jim A.

Library of Congress Catalog Card Number 94-73968

10 9 8 7 6 5 4 3

ISBN 0-9644887-4-4

Third Printing 1998

Dedication

This book is dedicated to anyone who finds anything personally useful in it, and to my spouse Max who for years seemed to drive me to drink, and who now plays an even more important role in my recovery.

Acknowledgements

Of all the pages in this book, this is possibly the most difficult to write. Where do I stop once I start naming people who have contributed to my recovery and to the subsequent writing of this book? I'm not using my last name, do I use theirs?

I must at least mention Brad D., Diane C., Ed D., Emily S., Ira F., my sponsor Jack N., John L., Kelly L., Lou A., Pat I. and Sue W. For final editorial support and help with computing, typesetting, page layout, and the various aspects of self-publishing, I am particularly indebted to Bob L., Don D. and Jim A.

I'm also indebted to many people I could have and probably should have mentioned.

Let me simply say: *Thank you all. Thank you very, very much. Thank you, thank you, thank you.*

CONTENTS

Preface

Preface

Over and over in the early years of my sobriety, I heard the admonition, "Stick with the Winners, Stick with the Winners."

I decided to not only stick with the Winners, but to become one even though I wasn't sure what one was. So I asked Chuck C.

Surely, I thought, an old-timer like Chuck would know, but he surprised me by hesitating. Then he said, "I guess you have to die sober."

I wanted to be a Winner, but dying wasn't part of my plan. Having to die to gain recognition never appealed to me. So I decided to *live* sober.

I decided to become a Winner by being a successful member of Alcoholics Anonymous. My definition of "successful" varied from time to time, and often my goal presented quite a challenge. But I figured if sobriety weren't a struggle, there wouldn't be so many unrecovered alcoholics.

In sobriety, I have become convinced that:

1. *Alcoholism is a medical problem, truly a disease, not merely a psychiatric symptom.*

2. *Alcoholics Anonymous is a spiritual answer to that medical problem, and beautiful, permanent recoveries are to be expected;*
3. *There is much, much more to recovery and to the A.A. program than mere abstinence from alcohol;*
4. *Carrying the message of recovery is an extremely important aspect of A.A.'s spiritual answer; and,*
5. *The more one gives this message to others, the more one is privileged to keep it.*

Since retiring from the practice of medicine, I've made message-carrying my primary hobby. I carry the message by example, by participating at meetings, by talking to "program people" between meetings, and by writing. Oddly enough, by doing these things I find out who I really am.

Writing about my twenty-seven years of sobriety and fifty-five years of marriage will help clarify my thinking, and I will almost certainly grow emotionally and spiritually while writing. I hope you do the same while reading.

I have the same hope for persons with addictions other than to alcohol. I trust they will accept my use of the words "alcohol" and "alcoholic" in a generic sense to cover all addictions.

For physical sobriety, I had to give up drinking.

ONE

PHYSICAL SOBRIETY
Drinking

Is Alcoholism *Really* A Disease?

In 1956 the American Medical Association declared alcoholism a disease.

Not everyone agrees with that opinion. Some agree alcoholism is a disease but then act as if it were a psychiatric symptom or a personality disorder. Physicians are no better in this regard than the rest of the population. Although pleased when they make an early diagnosis of diseases such as cancer, diabetes or high blood pressure, they often delay the label "alcoholic" until the patient's whole neighborhood knows the diagnosis.

All my life people have been telling me alcoholics are weak-willed. I grew up in a neighborhood drug store during the Great Depression. Hobos from the brickyard on the other side of the railroad track would come in to buy Sterno canned heat because of its wood alcohol content. My father refused to sell it to them. He called them drunken bums, and said they strained the Sterno through bread in an effort to remove the poisonous effects of the wood alcohol. In his opinion, they drank instead of facing up to their problems like real men should.

In pharmacy school, medical school and all my years of medical practice and continuing medical education, alcoholism was always presented as a psychiatric problem. The recommended treatment never changed: Give sedatives to the mild cases and refer the rest to psychiatrists, even though psychiatrists didn't like to treat alcoholics because of the poor recovery rate.

Recently, I heard a recovering alcoholic psychiatrist tell his story at my A.A. home group. He stressed in minute detail how he, in his opinion, drank because of his psychiatric problems. He related that he had received many years of psychotherapy plus extensive psycho-analysis for these problems, but he continued to drink.

As he continued to talk, I wondered: if alcoholism is a symptom of a psychiatric problem, why do psychiatrists become alcoholics? Why do psychiatrists have to come to A.A.? Why can't psychiatrists teach alcoholics how to not drink? Or how to drink in moderation?

Controlled drinking doesn't work for alcoholics. Neither does abstinence. That's alcoholism. *Alcoholics can't drink and they can't not drink.* While they can drink sensibly on occasion, they can't do so consistently. And, while they can abstain from drinking for a time, they can't do so persistently and comfortably.

Many diseases such as heart attacks, strokes, and epilepsy are easily recognized as diseases by their spectacular symptoms. Others run their course without displaying such drama.

Lung cancer, for instance, begins as a silent, microscopic speck in a person's lung and remains hidden until the day an x-ray examination reveals a small, ill-defined, gray, cloudy area of only questionable importance. Eventually the patient ends up in the mortuary.

At what point did the speck become what we think of as a disease? And at what point in its development does alcoholism become a disease? And, if alcoholism isn't a disease, what kills alcoholics? A weak will? A bad habit? Stupidity?

I choose to believe alcoholism begins as far back as a disease possibly can — at conception. Alcoholism hides in the alcoholic's genes and manifests itself as an abnormal reaction to alcohol.

I believe alcoholics drink to relieve completely unrecognized early withdrawal symptoms. Relief from these symptoms makes them feel *especially* good when they drink. Habitual cigarette smokers get a similar effect when they light up. Both are yielding to their addiction without realizing what they are doing.

I don't agree with those outside and inside A.A. who claim alcoholics drink merely to feel good. That's an unrealistic oversimplification. I refuse to believe we do all the harm we do to ourselves and to others simply to feel good, simply for the fun of it. Far too much of our drinking isn't fun. Quite the contrary.

One of the most exciting concepts during my medical career has been the realization that alcoholism is not merely a symptom of a psychiatric problem. It is a distinct disease in its own right.

Indeed, in my experience, alcoholism shows little response to the usual psychiatric methods and practically none to Freudian psychoanalysis and other approaches that seek to find out *why* the patient drinks.

Why*Do*Alcoholics Drink?

I n the beginning, we alcoholics may start drinking for pleasure or for social reasons or for any of the countless other reasons people in our culture drink alcohol. But how do we explain our inability to learn from the trouble caused by our drinking?

Do we continue to drink long after we've had enough simply because we're having so much fun? Why can't we stop? Why is alcohol so important to us? Are we to believe we are so stupid and selfish as to give up the house, car, kids, spouse, job, health, life itself, just for the fun of it? That's ridiculous. There simply has to be more to our disease than that.

In the early years of my working as a physician in the field of chemical dependency, a group of excited patients came to me to settle an argument. One of the group insisted that a perfectly normal, well-adjusted, emotionally mature individual could become an alcoholic if he or she drank. The rest of the group wanted me to tell him he was wrong. Instead, I agreed with him.

I believe anyone who has the appropriate genetic makup can become an alcoholic if adequately exposed to alcohol.

Alcoholism occurs in all sorts of people including even those who, until alcoholism develops, have no serious emotional problems. No class of individuals, financial, social, educational, intellectual, cultural or otherwise, is immune to alcoholism.

The only requirement for alcoholism is an abnormal reaction to alcohol. This abnormality develops either early or late in the alcoholic's drinking career.

In our culture, non-alcoholics drink alcohol for all sorts of reasons: as a social lubricant; because of peer pressure; or to participate in a wedding, funeral or party. Others drink to quench their thirst, to relax, to sleep, to relieve pain, to gain weight, to find false courage or for no particular reason at all.

Alcoholics drink for all the same reasons plus one additional reason more important than all the others combined: the disease, alcoholism, makes them drink.

In truth, it matters little why alcoholics drink or even how much they drink. It's what alcohol does to them that matters.

Alcoholics react differently to alcohol than do social drinkers.

Furthermore, they are totally unaware of this difference. Indeed, they commonly see alcohol as the answer rather than as the cause of their problems. This abnormal effect of alcohol on alcoholics eventually makes them (if they weren't already) neurotic, confused, insecure, frightened, even insane.

In the end, this so-called alcoholic personality is thought to have caused the disease, whereas it has, in fact, resulted from it. When a person describes himself or herself by saying, "I was an alcoholic long before I took the first drink," I understand them to mean that, in their opinion, they were emotionally disturbed before they started drinking.

Alcoholism is an abnormal reaction, an undesirable side effect, an allergy, if you will, to the drug, alcohol. The chemical, alcohol, reacts abnormally with the chemicals called the neurotransmitters [1] of the brain in such a way as to create a demand for alcohol. In time, this develops into recognizable craving and addiction.

This chemical change occurs at such a deep level that the alcoholic doesn't realize it has taken place. This inability of alcoholics to see that they react differently to alcohol than do social drinkers is called denial. However, the alcoholic is not lying. In spite of outward appearances, alcoholics do not realize their relationship with alcohol is abnormal. Ask alcoholics why they drink and they'll give you reasons ranging from plausible to ridiculous. Only rarely do they realize they drink because they must. Alcoholics actually *need* alcohol, they don't merely want it.

For many years scientists thought of the brain as a giant supercomputer run by electricity. Now they realize it is also a factory manufacturing complex chemicals which determine, among other things, our thinking, our attitudes, our desires, our sanity, indeed our lives and who we are. Freud, in perhaps his only observation of any significance directly related to the field of alcoholism, allegedly said the day will come when we will realize that every thought is a chemical reaction.

It is generally agreed that alcoholics constitute approximately ten percent of the drinking population. Why they react to alcohol differently than the rest of the population is unknown, but heredity plays an important role. The degree of susceptibility varies considerably. Some react abnormally by getting drunk and experiencing a blackout during their first drinking episode. Others drink for many years before suffering obvious adverse reactions.

Regarding this unusual reaction of alcoholics to alcohol, the Big Book (the name alcoholics have lovingly given *Alcoholics Anonymous*, the basic text of A.A.) says:

> ". . . we who have suffered alcoholic torture must believe that the body of the alcoholic is quite as abnormal as his mind. It did not satisfy us to be told that we could not control our drinking just because we were maladjusted to life, that we were in full flight from life . . . we are sure that our bodies were sickened as well." [2]

> "We know that while the alcoholic keeps away from drink . . . he reacts much like other men. We are equally positive that once he takes any alcohol whatever into his system, something happens, both in the bodily and mental sense, which makes it virtually impossible for him to stop." [3]

> ". . . there are types entirely normal in every respect except in the effect alcohol has upon them. They are often able, intelligent, friendly people. All these, and many others, have one symptom in common: they cannot start

drinking without developing the phenomenon of craving. This phenomenon,
as we have suggested, may be the
manifestation of an allergy . . . ." [4]

At the time the book *Alcoholics Anonymous* was written, little or nothing was known about the chemistry of the brain. Also, the book wasn't written by men of medicine. If it weren't for these two facts, I suspect the Big Book would have stated that alcoholism is an "abnormal reaction to alcohol" or an "undesirable side effect of alcohol" rather than an "allergy" to it. Had this happened, alcoholism would more commonly be recognized today as just one of many hundreds of examples of diseases caused by an undesirable side effect of a medication.

All Medications Have Undesirable Side Effects

A lcohol is a liquid tranquilizer. From the medical standpoint, there is nothing unusual about claiming that alcohol addiction results from an undesirable reaction to the drug, alcohol.

All prescription medications have undesirable side effects. [5] Since alcohol affects mainly the brain, abnormal reactions to it show up there pre-dominantly.

Once we get into recovery, most of us recognize
our need to exercise caution when dealing with
doctors who want to give us mind-affecting
medications, but we give little thought to the risks
involved in using other prescription drugs.

In truth, not until after a medication has been
taken can a physician tell whether or not a patient
is going to show an unusual reaction to it and, if
so, which of the many possible reactions it will
be.

Prescription medications, while making patients
well, can also make them ill, and can do so either
while the drugs are being administered or after
they have been stopped. They can also cause more
serious illnesses than the one for which they were
prescribed. They can do this with or without
having had a beneficial effect on the original
disease. Any number of examples can be offered
to illustrate this point.

Linda G. discovered the dangers of routine
medications the hard way. Her case was reported
in the medical literature in 1977. [6] She was an
attractive, vivacious TV and movie actress until
she developed a mysterious illness which began
with fatigability and progressed through many
complications over a period of twelve years. Her
hair changed color several times, then fell out. She

lost weight and developed agonizing abdominal pains and severe generalized itching. Eventually one arm and then both legs became paralyzed.

Although Linda underwent 340 x-ray examinations and consulted a total of 22 California physicians, none could tell her what was wrong. Many insisted she was neurotic and would have to learn to live with her condition. This made her angry. She decided to find the answer herself. Because of her paralysis, friends had to carry her into the medical library where she spent many hours taking notes with her unparalyzed left hand.

Eventually Linda proved she was suffering from chronic lead poisoning! The source of the lead was a bone meal preparation prescribed twelve years earlier by the first of the 22 doctors. She recalled phoning this physician early in her illness saying she wasn't feeling better and being told, "double the dose" — the same inappropriate advice sometimes given tremulous patients trying to discontinue tranquilizers.

Jack M. is an asthmatic. In contrast to Linda, he discovered that a disease caused by a medication may not appear until years later. For a long time Jack was happy having his asthma controlled by cortisone. Now he's unhappy about the extremely painful way his bones crumble. His spine collapses abruptly, one vertebra at a time. He grows progressively shorter. He now looks up at people formerly shorter than he.

Jack and Linda are but two examples of persons taking a medication in all innocence, only to discover later that it has had a disastrous effect on their lives. Isn't this the same thing that happens to approximately ten percent of the people who drink alcohol?

Richard T. discovered that some medications, stopped abruptly, cause diseases that are worse than the one under treatment. When he developed chest pains, his doctor diagnosed angina and prescribed an appropriate medication and warned him to not stop it until told to do so. His chest discomfort subsided completely. When the prescription ran out he felt so good he forgot to have it refilled immediately, thus stopping the medication abruptly. Three days later, instead of having angina, he had a massive heart attack and died.

In a similar manner, abruptly stopping a tranquilizer after prolonged use can result in even more severe nervous symptoms than those for which the medication was prescribed in the first place. Indeed, convulsions may occur.

As we all know, the abrupt cessation of alcohol after a prolonged period of heavy drinking can result in these same symptoms — the so-called *shakes, whiskey fits* or *DT's.*

Furthermore, medications can cause the conditions for which they are prescribed. Sleeping pills cause insomnia. Pain pills cause pain. Pep pills cause fatigue. And alcohol and other tranquilizers cause nervousness.

The above are just a few of many thousands of possible examples of how prescription medications cause undesirable side effects. Is it any wonder then that alcohol, a no-longer prescribed medication, also shows undesirable side effects in many people?

Should we refuse all prescription medications? Of course not. Physicians and pharmacists constantly watch for undesirable drug reactions, and the United States Food and Drug Administration doesn't permit the sale of a medication unless its potential benefits, in their opinion, outweigh the potential risks.

In this regard, alcohol, if discovered today, would not be approved for medicinal use. By reacting adversely with the neurochemicals of the brain in genetically susceptible individuals, it causes monstrous problems in approximately ten percent of the people who drink it — much too high a risk for only questionable medical benefit.

What about illegal drugs? Here the risks, including the risk of addiction, surpass any conceivable medical value. While the Food and Drug Administration considers them too dangerous for physicians to prescribe, drug dealers dispense them with no concern regarding their safety. Is it any wonder we get into trouble by using them?

Basic Assumptions Regarding Alcoholism

No one knows the cause of alcoholism. That being the case, I am free to believe whatever I want. I don't even need others to agree with me. So, based on both my professional and personal experience, I choose to believe the following:

✓ There's more to the disease, alcoholism, than a bad habit or a stupid way of responding to life's problems;

✓ Physical symptoms referable to the liver and other organs of the body are caused by excessive drinking. However, excessive drinking is a symptom, not the cause of alcoholism;

✓ Alcoholism is a distinct disease. It results from a change in the chemistry of the brain, brought on in susceptible individuals by alcohol or related chemicals;

✓ This chemical change accounts for the insanity of the alcoholic's drinking and explains why common sense, psychotherapy and tranquilizers don't correct the problem. It also explains why alcoholics return to drinking for ridiculous reasons or no reason at all, and why they are as likely to drink when things are going well as when they are going badly;

✓ It also explains why alcoholics can never safely return to drinking even after years of psychiatric or medical care or recovery in A.A. The basic problem is apparently one of bad genes, not bad habits;

✓ The same sort of chemical change in the brain probably explains why ex-smokers return to chain-smoking after one cigarette, compulsive overeaters can't stop eating once they start, and the first drink gets an alcoholic drunk;

✓ The alcoholic's thinking is different, not necessarily because it has always been that way, but because of the covert effects of altered brain-chemistry;

✓ This altered brain chemistry is what is known as "alcoholism."

✓ Psychiatrists commonly use an approach similar to that of practicing alcoholics in that they administer mood- and mind-affecting chemicals to control feelings and thinking. In nonalcoholic patients, who react to these drugs normally, this approach can be effective; but in alcoholics, who react differently, it can be disastrous;

✓ The psychiatric problems seen in alcoholics are more often the result than the cause of alcoholism. If a so-called "alcoholic personality" emerges, it does so after the disease has developed. If this were not so, it would be possible by psychological testing to prevent alcoholism by identifying and treating pre-alcoholics, and NASA would not have sent to the moon a man who later developed alcoholism.

✓ Once alcoholics start solving their living problems by turning to alcohol, they cease growing emotionally. As a result, if they didn't have emotional problems before they started drinking, they develop them once alcohol begins to exert its covert and peculiar effects on them.

Why Alcoholics Return To Drinking

There is a riddle about alcoholism that has never been explained: Since alcoholics can't control how much they drink once they start, why do they start?

I like to speculate that the answer lies hidden in the geography of the brain, the specific areas where each brain function is located.

Knowledge of brain topography is basic for brain surgeons. Without it, they could not cut into the brain without causing more harm than benefit. There is, for example, a center for speech, a center for the emotions, and an area where memories are stored. Separate centers control our ability to see, to breathe, and to move. Scientists have identified many such areas and they discover new ones all the time.

I visualize the brain as containing three such centers that are closely interconnected: an addiction center, a spiritual center, and a center for the emotions. These centers are highly dependent upon each other. High levels of activity in the spiritual center supress activity in the addiction center. These same high levels of spiritual energy stimulate the center for the emotions and increase the output of positive emotions while decreasing the output of negative emotions.

In alcoholics, activity in the addiction center means an increasing need for a drink. However, the addiction center does not have a direct connection to the thinking part of the brain. As a result, it cannot effectively communicate its need for a drink. Instead, the energy in the addiction center spreads to the nearby center for the emotions. This center then tells the brain something is wrong.

Because the message arrives from the center for the emotions, the brain interprets it as an emotional problem rather than as an addiction problem. As a result, the alcoholic thinks his or her spouse, job or circumstances made him or her drink.

Thinking is extremely important in this flow of energy. We can, by our thinking, exercise more control over our spiritual center than over our emotional center. Alcoholics can, for example, overcome fear more effectively by deciding to trust in God than by deciding to not be afraid. [7]

I like the way this theory of three interdependent centers harmonizes with the A.A. program. The A.A. way of life energizes both the spiritual center and the center for the emotions. These then suppress the addiction center. As a result, the alcoholic finds it surprisingly easy to stay sober. As the Big Book puts it, *"What we really have is a daily reprieve contingent on the maintenance of our spiritual condition."*[8]

The theory explains other things as well. As mentioned before, the addiction center can't communicate directly with the mind. It sends it's message by way of the center for the emotions. Because the message arrives via this route, it is not possible for the alcoholic or for anyone else to know whether the alcoholic is drinking for emotional reasons or because of pressure from the addiction center.

This uncertainty is the so-called "invisible line" which separates social drinking from alcoholism. In addition, the theory provides an explanation of much of the insanity of alcoholism, particularly the insanity of the first drink.

My theory of the three brain centers also explains why simply quitting drinking doesn't cure alcoholism. On the contrary, the addiction center becomes active in the absence of alcohol.

Perhaps some day a means will be found to quiet the addiction center. Until then, alcoholics will continue to suppress its activity by stimulating the spiritual center.

Progressing In Sobriety

In summary, alcoholism is a disease, a medical problem. Alcoholics can't consistently stop drinking after the first drink, and can't persistently keep from starting. To varying degrees, they have literally lost the power of choice as to whether or not they will drink and how much they will drink. Permanent changes took place in the chemistry of their brain when they added alcohol to their genetic susceptibility.

Neither they, nor alcohol, are unique in this matter. All drugs and all medications produce unusual responses in a certain percentage of people.

The physical discomfort associated with alcoholism disappears when the alcoholic quits drinking. The thinking problems and the emotional discomfort (both that which preceded the drinking and that which developed as a result of the unrecognized, unusual response to alcohol) persist for a considerably longer period of time. Until these are dealt with properly, long-term, comfortable sobriety is impossible.

Thus far, we have discussed only the drinking part of alcoholism. The thinking part is almost equally important, and is the subject of the next chapter.

References:

1. For an excellent discussion of brain chemistry, see Solomon H. Snyder, *Drugs And The Brain*, (New York City: Scientific American Library; 18, 1986).

2. *Alcoholics Anonymous*, 3rd ed. (New York City: Alcoholics Anonymous World Sevices,Inc., 1976), p. xxiv (with permission).

3. ibid. p. 22–23.

4. ibid. p. xxviii.

5. *PDR Physicians' Desk Reference*, (Montvale, NJ: Medical Economics Data Production Company, 1994), bulges with examples of reactions to prescription medications.

6. William H. Crosby M.D., "Lead Contaminated Health Food", *The Journal of the American Medical Association*, 237, No. 24 (June 1977), p. 2627.

7. See the next chapter.

8. *Alcoholics Anonymous*, 3rd ed. (New York City: Alcoholics Anonymous World Services, Inc., 1976), p. 85 (with permission).

*For mental sobriety, I had to give up letting my
mind control itself — and me!*

TWO

MENTAL SOBRIETY
Thinking

The Thinking Part of Alcoholism

When I first came to A.A., few things bothered me more than the way people kept talking about drinking. That's all they talked about. I wanted to talk about problems; they wanted to talk about drinking.

Today, I see it their way. They were comparing their behavior while drinking to the behavior of society in general, but at that time my thinking kept me from hearing what they were saying. So I kept on drinking.

I couldn't stop drinking until I first stopped thinking. I finally gave up my way of thinking about life and its problems, and, without waiting to evaluate their recommendations, I took the actions suggested by my sponsor and by those who got sober before me. This is "surrender." Without it, alcoholics can't recover.

In sobriety, although alcoholics return to thinking, they can't return to their old ways of thinking. If they do, they end up like the alcoholic described in the Big Book. Having just finished lunch in a restaurant, the man said, "Suddenly the thought crossed my mind that if I were to put an ounce of whiskey in my milk, it couldn't hurt me on a full stomach." [1] Within a short period of time he was, of course, drunk.

Such self-destructive, weird and circuitous thinking is common in alcoholics. An alcoholic living in a recovery home once told me he'd spent the day looking for a job. "I needed the money," he said. He'd traveled by bicycle because he'd lost his car. The recovery home was on top of a hill and the day was hot and sunny. When he became tired and sweaty he thought of a cold beer. "I'd have stopped and bought one," he said, "but I had no money."

Some years ago, I treated a totally surrendered skid row alcoholic at Long Beach General Hospital. In the detox unit after fifteen years of hard drinking, he was entirely willing to do anything suggested in order to get well. However, a mere six days later, he stood in the hallway smoking cigarettes and swapping tales with two of his peers as several of us passed him on our way to the auditorium. I called out, "Come on, Bill. It's time for the A.A. meeting." Without the slightest pause, he bellowed, "Hell, I don't need that crap!" Already he had "dissurrendered." He had returned to relying on his alcoholic brain to keep him sober, the same brain that kept him drunk.

Alcoholics can't survive without thinking. And they can't survive if they continue their old ways of thinking.

My Alcoholic Brain

Thinking has always been a problem for me. If my only problem had been drinking, I could have handled it easily. If drinking is a problem, don't drink. I knew that. But my common sense and good intentions dissolved when drinking and thinking joined forces against me.

My brain and my body have always been in conflict. My mind has always wanted things my body can't provide. They never agreed on whether or not we could drink. My body told my brain, "Alcohol gives us high blood pressure, diabetes, a peptic ulcer and colitis. It sickens our liver and unpredictably switches our mind off and on for variable periods of time. It causes mental confusion amounting to a toxic psychosis. We almost always walk and talk funny when we drink. We simply do *not* handle alcohol well."

After a moment or two of thoughtful consideration, my brain responded with, "Oh well, what the hell! One little drink never hurt anybody."

It's not that I was weak-willed. It's just that my mind has a mind of its own, and it changed its mind. Not having a drink was no longer important.

In addition, my mind habitually lied to me. One little drink was all it ever wanted. But soon after it got the first drink, it began to chant, "Just one more." Alcohol didn't quench my mind's thirst; it increased it. As a result, over and over again I found myself drinking more than I should have, even at times when I hadn't intended to drink at all.

Further evidence of alcoholic thinking appears in the affirmative answers when the word "thinking" is substituted for "drinking" in the twenty questions published by Johns Hopkins Hospital.

Are You an Alcoholic?

1. Do you lose time from work due to your thinking?
2. Is your thinking making your home life unhappy?
3. Do you think because you are shy with other people?
4. Is your thinking affecting your reputation?
5. Have you ever felt remorse after thinking?
6. Have you gotten into financial difficulty as a result of thinking?
7. Do you turn to lower companions or an inferior environment when thinking?
8. Does your thinking make you careless of your family's welfare?
9. Has your ambition decreased since thinking?
10. Do you crave a think at a definite time daily?
11. Do you want to think the next morning?
12. Does thinking cause you to have difficulty in sleeping?
13. Has your efficiency decreased since thinking?
14. Is thinking jeopardizing your job or business?
15. Do you think to escape from worries or trouble?
16. Do you think alone?
17. Have you ever had a complete loss of memory as a result of thinking?
18. Has your physician ever treated you for thinking?
19. Do you think to build up your self-confidence?
20. Have you ever been to a hospital or institution on account of your thinking?

After listing these questions in their usual form using "drinking" instead of "thinking," Johns Hopkins Hospital says: "If you have answered YES to any one of these questions, there is a definite warning that you may be an alcoholic. If you have answered YES to any two, the chances are that you are an alcoholic. If you have answered YES to three or more, you are definitely an alcoholic."

How's *your* thinking?

When I was drinking and my body complained about the bad effects alcohol had on us, my mind would agree. "You're right," it would say. "This is definitely not good for us. We're going to knock it off. Forever! However, since we're already drinking today, it's no use quitting now. We'll quit tomorrow. First thing in the morning."

Having definitely established the exact date and time for quitting, we were now free to go on drinking tonight. Especially since these would be the last drinks we would ever have.

Today I use that same thinking process to stay sober. I tell myself, "This is an important day for me. Today is the day I don't drink. I drank many a yesterday and I'm going to drink tomorrow, but I don't drink today." I'd probably not be able to keep from drinking today if I didn't know I was going to drink tomorrow. When tomorrow gets here, I'll check the time. If it's today, I won't drink today.

We Are Responsible For Our Thoughts

In *Change Your Voice, Change Your Life,*[2] Morton Cooper points out how, as children, we learn to speak, and seldom thereafter question the effectiveness or even the pleasantness of our voice. Some of us, he points out, speak too loudly, some too softly; some too fast and some too slowly. One person's pitch is too high. Another starts talking before his partner has finished speaking. Still others appear speechless.

Until recovery, I paid little more attention to my thinking than to my voice. I have no idea when I first learned to think, but having learned, I turned my mind loose to roam around aimlessly like an adolescent looking for trouble. I didn't realize the important role my thinking played in determining both the quality and the course of my life.

Neither did I understand my responsibility regarding its behavior. I assumed everyone's mind ran on automatic pilot. I had choices but didn't know it. Indeed, until I learned I had a choice, I didn't really have a choice. Today I accept the concept that while I am not responsible for all the ideas that fly into my head, I am responsible for those I entertain there.

Like a powerful searchlight or laser beam, thinking should be aimed with care. Eye surgeons use laser beams in short bursts to destroy unwanted blood vessels in the retina of the eye. Because of its power, the beam could drill a hole through both the patient and the operating table. Extreme care must be exercised in aiming the gun and fingering the trigger. Thinking is equally as powerful. And as dangerous. But not as accurately controllable.

My thinking not only controls my life, it determines who I am. Brian Tracy points this out in his audiocassette series, *The Psychology of Achievement*[3] when he says, "You are not what you think you are, but what you think, you are."

My Mind vs My Computer

My mind has a defective toggle switch. It indiscriminately turns itself off and on, thinks when it should be resting, rests when it should be thinking, and thinks about things it should ignore. Like an ultraviolet light, it stimulates the growth of much that it shines on. The longer it focuses on good things, the better they become — writing a gratitude list makes me grateful. The longer my mind dwells on bad things, the worse they become — resentments increase in size and become "justifiable."

A humorist once remarked that he could have made some useful suggestions if he'd been around at the time of Creation. If I'd been there, I'd have suggested that my brain be more like my computer. As computers become more powerful, people who know about such things wonder if computers will ever match the capabilities of the human brain. I think the answer is obvious. Even now, my computer could give my brain a few lessons, especially in matters such as dependability, efficiency and user-friendliness.

If I had my way, my mind, in addition to an On/Off switch, would have Erase, Delete and Rewind capabilities. When I type "CLS" on my computer, the screen clears itself of whatever we've been working on, and we start over fresh. In fact, when totally confused and not sure what to do next, my computer stops. It refuses to move in any direction. To get it to start over with not a single memory of the confusion, I press Control+Alt+Delete. The screen goes blank. The machine discards all the clutter. In a few seconds it lights up and, in effect, says, "I'm ready now. Let's start over."

I learned how to get my computer to do this by reading the owner's manual. Not only can my mind not clear itself of confusion in such an efficient manner, it came with no operating instructions and no manufacturer's guarantee. I'm completely on my own in trying to figure out how to use it.

Never, after turning my computer off before going to bed, have I known it to turn itself on in the middle of the night and resume work on a problem we struggled with earlier in the evening. My mind, having a mind of its own, does this all the time.

When I finish a project on my computer it asks, "Do you want to save this?" A "Yes" response guarantees the material will be saved and returned to me later. But only if I request it. And precisely as written. Not a word, not a punctuation mark altered.

My mind doesn't comprehend such servility. It insists on its right to an opinion as to what we will remember and what we will forget. Without any hesitation or explanation, it discards information it doesn't like and remembers facts that aren't so. And when I complain, it argues with me.

I choose the program my computer and I are going to work with depending on what I want to accomplish. I choose a word processor program to process words, a number processor program for numbers, an idea processor for ideas, or a data processor for data. My computer always agrees with my choice, and that's what we work on until I decide to do something different.

Not so my mind. My mind jumps from one totally unrelated subject to another with no regard for anything else. Later, considering all the effort we put into the project, it wonders why we accomplished so little.

The Noise

Furthermore, while my computer gives off a rather pleasant, mild, steady hum, my brain commonly puts out ceaseless chatter of varying intensity. Before I realized what was going on, this drove me to drink.

In sobriety I've come to realize that my mind talks to me. It talks all the time, day and night. It doesn't do any physical work, it just talks. Talk, talk, talk, talk. And by its talking, it controls my thinking, my feelings, my actions — my life.

In years past, I tried to control the talking with chemicals. Today I avoid all mind-affecting substances. Even a mild drug like caffeine stimulates the talk to talktalktalktalk, and at bedtime when my body wants to go to sleep, my mind insists, "No, let's lie here and talk awhile."

After I get to sleep, around 3:00 a.m. it sometimes shouts, "Hey, wake up! We've had an emergency meeting up here and we need to talk to you. You know that situation you thought you handled so well today? Well, it wasn't like that at all! People are really upset with you. Wait till morning. You'll find out!"

I decide to not listen to such nonsense. I roll over and go back to sleep. Just as I'm about to lose consciousness, I think, "Boy, I'm sure glad I'm not thinking about that any more." But my mind hears me thinking and calls out, "Oh, I'm glad you're still awake. You know, that's not the only dumb thing you've done. You did the same thing about six months ago. In fact, you've done a lot of dumb things in your life. Let's spend the rest of the night lying here making a list of all the dumb things you've done. You must be one of the dumbest people we've ever met."

Sometimes this chatter goes on while I sleep, and I awaken in the morning feeling anxious or confused, my day ruined before it has started. I decided this morning discomfort results from conversations that go on in my head during unremembered dreams. Evening meetings come too late in the day to take care of this problem, so I convinced friends to help me start a meeting the first thing in the morning, seven days a week.

We call them "Attitude Adjustment Meetings." The format includes the statement, "This is not a meeting devoted so much toward reliving the past as toward developing the appropriate attitudes for living this particular day successfully." They are topic-discussion meetings, and they've changed my life. If you have a problem like mine, try morning meetings. But be careful; they're quite addictive.

The Committee In My Head

Any time I'm alone with my mind, I'm outnumbered. Unsupervised, my mind consists of a talkative, rowdy, unorganized group of personalities with no apparent plan or sense of direction. Until recovery, I hadn't realized that, at birth, I was expected to assume the role of chairman of the group. We, the personalities and I, traveled through life like a crowded tour bus with no driver. One of the passengers drove for a while in any direction. After a while, another passenger took over without talking to the first. Later, a third drove wherever he wanted until someone took over from him. Later, we all wondered why we never got anywhere.

We had a similar problem with drinking. In the morning, one of us would decide to quit drinking forever. In the evening, another of us, without talking to the first, would have a drink. I had a serious communication problem in that the different parts of my brain weren't talking to each other.

Few concepts have been more important to my long-term, total sobriety than the realization that my mind is composed of multiple personalities.

As a group, these personalities can't make sensible decisions unless I act as chairman and bring order to their meetings.

Each individual has a definite opinion and a narrow point of view. One, for example, is always afraid. No matter what action is suggested, if it is at all unfamiliar, he insists, "No, No, No! Don't do that! You'll screw it up and they'll all laugh at you!" He offers no other suggestion, ever.

Another personality has the opposite opinion. "Man," he says, "as long as you're sober, you can go anywhere, face anyone and do anything you want. There's no way anyone can harm you except to make you take a drink. And, as long as you have this program, no one can make you take a drink if you don't want to. You have absolutely *nothing* to fear, ever!"

One of them up there doesn't care much for Max, my wife. He never has. He obsessively watches her and reports back to me asking questions like, "Did you see what she just did? Are you going to let her speak to you in that tone of voice? Does she realize who she's talking to?"

Another personality thinks Max is wonderful. He points out how attractive she is and what a great sense of humor she has. He tells me how lucky I am to have a partner who, in the beginning, even though not alcoholic, went to A.A. meetings after I decided to quit, and who still attends A.A. meetings while remaining an active, participating, enthusiastic member of Al-Anon. Listening to this personality instead of the fault-finder has helped us stay happily (most of the time) married for over 55 years so far.

One lifelong problem in keeping the committee peaceful is the presence in my head of a cynical voice that passes judgment on everything that happens. It's like having a saboteur at the highest level of security where every piece of incoming information goes to his desk first. He stamps it with comments like, "This is unfair! This is awful! You shouldn't have to put up with this! Who do they think they're talking to? You're being taken again! Don't let them get away with this!"

He, like the personality who specializes in justifying resentments, loves his work. He takes pride in his ability to pick out the flaw, the defect, the fault, the things that are wrong with people, places, things and situations. And he delights in pointing them out to me. As a result, very little entered my life before the program without first being judged bad, frightening, or dangerous. This kept me in the role of victim with the attitude: "See how difficult my life is compared to other people. You mustn't expect too much of me."

Of all the personalities in my head, only one, thank God, is alcoholic.

He has a loud mouth and a pushy personality. With the slightest provocation, or none at all, he shouts, "Hey! Let's have a drink!" I used to pay a lot of attention to him, and he often got me drunk when I wasn't even thinking about drinking.

Now that I realize who is talking, instead of hearing his comment as a command, I take it as a mere suggestion. I consider the source, remember what it used to be like, and say, "Thank you for your participation. Now if you'll sit down, we'll call on someone else." He grumbles a bit, moves to the back of the room, and waits for his next opportunity.

He's the only personality in my head who likes to see me drink. The others want me sober.

I've discovered two important factors that influence my conversations with the personalities in my head.

First, getting angry really stimulates them. They love to argue. Second, the personalities I listen to the most move to the front of the room where they dominate our conversations and talk the loudest and the longest. Those I ignore drift to the rear and tend to remain quiet. No one ever leaves. The alcoholic personality will always be there waiting to speak up as soon as he thinks I might be in the mood to listen and to carry on a conversation with him.

The Center of Calm

In contrast to the surrounding noise, in the deepest part of me, in the last place I would have thought to look, I've discovered a Center of Calm, an area of peace, joy and serenity. My Higher Power resides there. He always has, but I didn't know it. And not knowing God is within is a lot like not having a Personal God.

My situation is not unique. Our Higher Power resides in the center of each of us. Check it out the next time you wake in the middle of the night, or while sitting quietly during a meeting. Or, at the end of a meeting during the prayer, instead of closing your eyes or looking at the floor, look around the room into the eyes of other alcoholics. Notice how you smile instinctively when your Higher

Power recognizes the Higher Power in the other person.

After finding God in the center of me, I decided to become friendly with the various personalities in my head. I've learned to love them even when I dislike their behavior. When their suggestions are impractical, unwise, silly, even lewd or illegal, I realize their intentions are good. They, like so-called "dysfunctional" parents, are trying to help me in the only way they know how. I no longer fight them, nor do I demand their silence.

Neither do I let them fight among themselves. Instead, I have them talk and write letters back and forth to each other and to me. They've quieted down considerably since learning to freely express their fears and emotions.

And since my Higher Power and I now generally act together as chairmen of the group, they are happier and function more efficiently. We listen to their suggestions. Then my Higher Power and I decide what we as a group are going to do, and what we are going to think about. Formerly, as mentioned earlier, all decisions were left to the personalities that shouted the loudest.

According to the Law of Appreciation, [4] whether we realize it or not, each of us determines the quality of our lives by choosing our thoughts. The

Law of Appreciation states that absolutely nothing on earth is totally good or totally bad. Good and bad coexist according to the Law, in every person, place, thing, law, situation, institution, or combination thereof.

In addition, it says that by focusing our attention on the good, we make the good better, and by focusing on the bad we make the bad worse. Thus, people who complain always have something to complain about, and people who smile always have something to smile about. They're both right.

> *It's as though our thoughts have energy, and, whether for good or evil, we transfer that energy into the subject of our thoughts.*

Worry puts energy into the problem; prayer and meditation put energy into the program.

Insisting that we can think only one thought at a time, author Emmet Fox suggested what he called The Golden Key [5] as the solution to any problem. He claimed that any problem, no matter how big or how small, can be "Golden Key'd." He described the method as substituting a spiritual thought the minute the problem comes to mind. For example, instead of thinking about the problem, immediately and repeatedly recite the Serenity Prayer or a favorite spiritual axiom such as, "If God be with me, who can be against me?" Ultimately, the bigger the problem, the higher the resultant level of spirituality of the person using this technique.

Problems

All my problems today are thinking problems. I don't even have a problem unless I think I do. If I think I have a problem, I have a problem; if I don't think I have a problem, I don't have a problem. Never have I thought I had a problem and been wrong.

Not only do I alone decide whether or not I have a problem; I alone determine the size of my problems. I don't have many little problems; I don't bother with them. Like resentments, I stick to the "justifiable" variety. When I do have a little problem, all I have to do to make it a big problem is to think about it.

As a boy, I read in *Reader's Digest* that you can judge a man by what makes him angry. From then on I searched for problems worthy of my anger. As a physician, I dedicated my life to working on problems, my own or anyone else's. I became a problem-magnet. When I couldn't find enough of my own, I borrowed yours. "My, that's an interesting problem you have there; may I have it for a while?" Meanwhile, I exaggerated, inflated and manufactured problems while remaining on the lookout for more. And I always found them.

I was like the young woman at an Al-Anon meeting who said her father told her as a child, "Most of the things we worry about don't happen." So, ever an obedient child, she established a worry policy. She protected herself by worrying about things in order to keep them from happening. She displayed the kind of logic that says, "Most auto accidents occur within twenty miles of your home — so move!"

Until recovery, I too believed in the positive power of worry. I believed worry, like an invisible plastic shield, kept problems from getting to me. If they did get through or over to me, I didn't feel guilty because I knew I'd done my best.

Problems have always enjoyed a position of exaggerated importance in my life. Early on, I came to the conclusion that the people with the most problems get the most attention. People don't want to hear how easy your life is; they want to hear about problems. The TV evening news stresses nothing else. Facing problems is the stuff of which heroes are made. Without problems you wouldn't have an identity. How can people think of you as being heroic if they don't know you're surviving in spite of it all? So tell them. Whine a little.

I grew up thinking all men of intelligence and stamina worked on their problems by thinking about them until they came up with an answer. I've discovered that approach works the opposite for me. Problems I think about grow bigger and bigger. Even non-problems. At first I'll think, "Well, that's certainly not a problem." But in a short time I can see where, "It could be sort of a problem." Soon I'm thinking, "Say, this is a bit of a problem." In no time I'm telling myself, "By golly, it's a good thing I'm looking at this. Everyone else is missing it."

One of the problems with problems is their high infant mortality rate. Ignored, they, like delicate plants, wither and die. Problems need a continuous flow of conversation, plus lots of water and fertilizer — especially fertilizer. They demand constant attention. Problems need to feel important.

Have you ever had a problem so delicate you couldn't leave it long enough to go to a meeting? "Tonight is meeting night. Are you going to be there?" "Oh no, I have to stay home and work on my problem." You know if you waste time going to a meeting, by the time you get back, your problem may have wilted to the point where you might not be able to bring it back.

Problems refuse to be ignored. When we work with newcomers and other alcoholics, they disappear. They get bored waiting and leave to find someone willing to give them the uninterrupted attention they demand. In general, we do the same thing. Most often, we don't solve our problems; we merely tire of them and move on to something else.

Think–Do–Feel

In years past I often watched myself as I behaved in a totally unacceptable manner — drinking, slamming doors, saying things I didn't want to say, doing things I didn't want to do. As a practicing alcoholic, I lacked self-control.

Today I see myself as a spiritual being with three distinct human facets: I am what I think; I am what I do; I am what I feel. And, to the degree that I control my thinking, I control my actions. To the degree that I control both my thinking and my actions, I control my feelings. Then, the circle is completed when my feelings affect my thinking which again affects my actions.

I might, for example, think to myself, "I'd like to do something nice for Max; I'll buy her some flowers." My thinking has inspired me to take an action. As a consequence of buying the flowers, I feel good.

Indeed, I feel so good I think, "That was a good idea; I'll do it again soon."

Of the three: thinking, actions and feelings, actions are, in many respects, the most important.

As Clancy I. has said at meetings, "They don't lock us up for thinking crazy; they only lock us up for acting crazy." We may, for example, think obsessively about drinking, and we may dream drinking dreams, but we don't lose our sobriety unless we pick up a drink and drink it. People see us as alcoholics because of our drinking, not because of our thinking.

I recall a girl at an A.A. meeting saying she couldn't see why people thought she was an alcoholic until she realized they were judging her by her actions while she was judging herself by her intentions. Like her, I always focused proudly on my good intentions, my thinking, while excusing my behavior.

In A.A. we frequently hear action slogans such as: Keep coming back; Action is the magic word; Bring the body and the mind will follow; You can't think yourself into right acting, but you can act your way into right thinking; Sit down, shut up and listen.

Such action-based admonitions are intended to get new people to take specific actions without thinking, without judging the value of the suggestion.

Indeed, Robyn Dawes, after criticizing much of modern psychiatric theory, ends her book *House of Cards* [6] with the statement, "Most important of all, there is no evidence that for the majority of people a change of internal state and feeling is necessary prior to behaving in a beneficial way. There is, in contrast, good evidence that changing our behavior will change our internal state and feelings. *Just do it*." (Emphasis added.)

However, any action more complicated than a simple knee-jerk response must be preceded by a thought, even if the thought is as simple as, "Okay, I'll do it." Actions require at least minimal thinking.

My actions are determined by my thinking, and I alone am responsible for my thinking. Furthermore, since my thinking and my actions determine my feelings, I am responsible for my feelings.

I can't honestly say, "You made me angry!" If you do something offensive and I become upset by thinking how selfish and inconsiderate you are, my thinking upsets me, not your behavior. I may tell you I am upset, but I must realize my being upset comes from me, not out of you or your behavior.

This is the basis of the statement in *The Twelve Steps And Twelve Traditions* [7] that says, "It is a spiritual axiom that every time we are disturbed, no matter what the cause, there is something wrong *with us.*"

Because of my frequent failure to remember this axiom and to control my thinking, I have given the entire matter to my Higher Power. First, I reminded Him of my powerlessness and the unmanageability of my life; then, I turned over to His care, not only my will and my life, but everything I think, feel and do.

He handles it all quite well most of the time, but on occasion I've had to reprimand Him. "For God's sake, God, what did You have me say (do, think, feel) that for? Are You paying any attention up there?" (If nothing else, this policy gives me someone with whom to share the blame when I function in a bizarre manner.)

We hear a lot about feelings these days. They're all the rage in mental health counseling. Feel your feelings, give them a name, and express them instead of acting them out. That's the message of the therapists. Just as Christians have many religious sects to choose from, so psychotherapists have at least 400 different schools of therapy to consider. Additional methods continue to evolve, while Freudian psychoanalysis with its ruminations about the past continues to fade in popularity.

One of the most practical of these newer methods is cognitive (thinking) therapy. To use this technique, clients begin by becoming aware of their thinking, that is, their inner conversations with themselves. Then, by writing out their thoughts, they learn to change their thinking. Doctor David Burns effectively treats depression in this manner. He explains the method in *Feeling Good, The New Mood Therapy*. [8]

Another psychotherapeutic technique, one that deals almost exclusively with the present, is that of psychiatrist William Glasser. Both his method and his book are entitled *Reality Therapy*. [9] Glasser teaches his clients to think, behave and feel realistically towards the reality of their current life rather than to dwell on their past life. In his lectures, Glasser points out the foolishness of clients who, instead of working to change themselves, want others, usually their parents, to change, and want them to do it now, retroactively, in spite of the fact that they are often long since dead.

These are but two examples of psychological approaches designed to change thinking in order to change feelings. In the next and subsequent chapters, we'll discuss additional methods for maintaining emotional sobriety.

Attitudes And Beliefs

Over the years I've learned quite a bit from various psychiatrist and psychologist friends and writers, yet for some reason I was particularly impressed on a Sunday morning at the Ohio Street meeting in Los Angeles when an A.A. member made the simple pronouncement, "Happiness is the absence of unhappiness."

Such a simple profundity, and yet I was startled. To be happy, merely stop finding reasons to be unhappy? All I have to do is change my thinking? My philosophy had always been, "You'd be unhappy too if you had my life. Let me tell you about it."

Today I realize that not only does my thinking control my feelings and my actions, it controls two additional extremely important facets of my personality: *My attitudes and my spiritual beliefs.* God doesn't exist in my life in a personal way unless I either decide to believe He exists, or decide to live my life *as if* I believed He exists. Either decision profoundly affects my attitude, and my attitude affects just about every aspect of my life.

Philosopher Baruch Spinosa didn't believe in the existence of God as a separate entity. He saw all objects, including humans, as part of God's self-expression. He thought of God as reality, as being identical with the world as we know it. At first, I discarded this as the thinking of an athiest. More recently I decided that, if, as the Bible says, God created the world in six days, rested for one, and has been busy creating reality ever since, then reality is the way in which God manifests Himself. In this sense then, reality is God, or is in this life all we will ever know of God .

My days, one at a time, consist of reality, created by God, plus my attitude, created by me. God and I are thus co-creators of my day.

The question becomes: Whose contribution is greater in determining the quality of my day? Most days it seems to be mine.

I believe that each day God gives me everything I need to have a good day. My choice of attitude determines whether or not I enjoy His gift. As someone said: It's hard to have a good day with a bad attitude, and it's hard to have a bad day with a good attitude. Every day is a good day. Whether or not I see it as such is up to me.

Progressing In Sobriety

Alcoholics are labeled "alcoholic" because of their behavior. Their behavior changes as they change their thinking. With a change in behavior and a change in thinking, it should be easy to stay sober. And it would be if we didn't have feelings, and if we didn't let other people control how we feel. Comfortable, long-term sobriety demands that we pay attention to this matter.

We'll talk about that next.

References:

1. *Alcoholics Anonymous*, 3rd ed. (New York City: Alcoholics Anonymous World Services, Inc. 1976), p. 36.

2. Morton Cooper, *Change Your Voice, Change Your Life*, (New York: Macmillan, 1984).

3. Brian Tracy, *The Psychology of Achievement*, audiocsassette series (Chicago: Nightingale-Conant Corporation.

4. David Goodman, *Living From Within*, (Kansas City, MO: Hallmark Editions, 1968), p. 7.

5. Emmet Fox, *Power Through Constructive Thinking*, (New York: Harper and Row, 1940), pp. 137-140.

6. Robyn M. Dawes, *House of Cards — Psychology And Psychotherapy Built On Myth*, (New York, The Free Press, a division of Macmillan, Inc, 1994), p. 293.

7. *The Twelve Steps and Twelve Traditions*, (New York City: Alcoholics Anonymous World Services, Inc., 1953), p. 92.

8. David D. Burns, M.D., *Feeling Good, The New Mood Therapy*, (New York: A Signet Book, New American Library, Times Mirror, 1980).

9. William Glasser, M.D., *Reality Therapy, A New Approach To Psychiatry*, (New York: Harper and Row, 1965).

For emotional sobriety, I had to give up letting others control my emotions.

THREE

EMOTIONAL SOBRIETY
Feeling

Who's In Charge Here?

Thanks to A.A., the people we alcoholics live with no longer drive us to drink. But some days they push us to the city limits where a lot of drinking takes place, and "dry drunks" turn into "slips." Yet, as often as I found myself out there on the outskirts of emotional sobriety, not once did I ask myself why I always accepted the role of passenger on these trips. It never occurred to me to do the driving myself, to take a leadership role and end up where I wanted to be rather than where someone was taking me.

When drinking, I often couldn't see that I wasn't physically sober. In recovery, I often can't see that I'm not emotionally sober. As when drinking, I don't recognize my change of personality. I think it's the other person who has changed, not me.

When I was drinking, I often got drunk when I didn't mean to, sometimes when I hadn't even planned on drinking. All sorts of situations, usually involving people, got me started. Not until I made a commitment to sobriety, not until I made it my top priority could I stay physically sober. That left me to deal with my emotions. I'd never put any great value on my emotional sobriety. I would often, in a sense, throw it at people who didn't want it and didn't know they had it — people on the freeway for instance.

Today I'm willing to go to any length, any length at all, to maintain my physical sobriety, and as time goes by, I'm willing to go to increasingly greater lengths to maintain my emotional sobriety.

It feels good to feel good. Besides, there's always that underlying possibility that if I lose my emotional sobriety badly enough and long enough, I might decide "Oh, what's the use?" and take a drink.

I don't want that to happen. It must feel awful to return to drinking and end up with a head full of A.A. and a belly full of booze. Certainly, it's no fun to be emotionally drunk with a head full of A.A. and a belly full of resentments.

"Success" Meant Control

In 1930 at age 12 during the Great Depression, I hurried home to tell my family I had negotiated the purchase of a newspaper route. I knew they'd be pleased and in later years would look back on this event as the beginning of what had become a vast financial empire.

Instead, my father was not pleased. No son of his would have an outside job. What would the neighbors and customers think if the son of the neighborhood druggist had to have a newspaper route to bring in extra money? My father would look like a failure! That, he could not allow.

Although I cancelled the purchase of the newspaper route, obeying my father was not my primary mistake.

More important was my acceptance of his value system which said other people's opinions of me were more important than my own.

Throughout my school years, all history classes gave recognition to the men and women who made a name for themselves by managing, controlling and affecting the lives of others. In and out of school I heard the message: To get anywhere, you've got to impress, control, manipulate, compete with, and at the same time get along with, the people in your life.

Look, for example, at the struggles between couples in relationships, between children and their parents, and between employees and their employers. Nations and politicians fight with each other all the time. Even members of so-called A.A. clubs can't always get along well together. Life apparently is a struggle for power: Either be in control or be controlled.

I Lost Control

Meanwhile, I couldn't control my drinking. I couldn't control it once I started, and I couldn't keep from starting. The more I lost control, the harder I fought for it. The more my disease extended into other areas of my life, the harder I fought to control the people, places, things and situations involved in the problem. I know now that this is rather typical behavior for an alcoholic.

I even continued my control efforts after being admitted as a patient to the mental health unit of a hospital of which I was a medical staff member. I spent my time in the psycho unit writing notes, letters and lists of things for my wife, Max, to do to keep the world running while I sat in a locked ward.

Today I can see that that didn't make much sense. On the other hand, neither did the fact that she returned of her own free will every day to pick up her list.

A.A. Doesn't Teach Control

In A.A., instead of hearing about control, I heard about powerlessness, unmanageability, surrender, acceptance, "Let go and let God." After seven months of this sort of indoctrination, I turned my critical judgment off and began to do the things my future sponsor and other sober alcoholics suggested as the way to stay sober. Among other things, I discovered that, just as drinking is an activity, so is sobriety.

According to our recovery program, powerlessness extends far beyond the question of drinking. The Steps declare our powerlessness over our own lives. The Traditions state that, being equal, no one of us has power over any of the rest of us. The Concepts state that Alcoholics Anonymous will never take punitive action in an effort to control any alcoholic. The Big Book says that we no longer fight any one or any thing.

In Al-Anon I heard someone say, "The more you try to control another person, the more you're under that person's control. If what you do next depends on whether they do or don't do whatever it is you are trying to get them to do or not do, then you are under that person's control."

All of this contradicts everything I already "knew" about life. I had always kept my focus out there on others, on people I didn't like, on people I resented. Then, as mentioned earlier, I heard a speaker in A.A. say, "Happiness is the absence of unhappiness," and I remembered Chuck C. repeatedly saying, "Happiness is an inside job." These thoughts combined with the idea that "A.A. stands for altered attitudes," launched me on a search for the mental, emotional and spiritual sobriety which lie on the far side of physical sobriety.

The Two-World Concept

Before I got to A.A., I was seriously confused. Eventually I realized that much of my confusion resulted not only from alcoholism but also from living simultaneously, without realizing it and without a road map, in two entirely different worlds — one outside and one inside my head.

We are spiritual beings, and we manifest our spirituality by our actions, by our thinking and by our feelings. These three areas are not equally represented in the two worlds. All our actions take place in the outer world, while our thoughts and feelings are confined to the secret, inner world. Thus, serenity and joy, plus all spiritual beliefs and feelings, and many of the most important things in life are exclusively inner-world matters.

In the other world, the world of reality, hard work often leads to success. In the world of the mind, however, working on a problem often leads to chaos. Although work works in the outside world, work that becomes worry commonly worsens situations in the inner world.

How does one learn to live comfortably and simultaneously in two different worlds? I began by paying attention from moment to moment to whether I am thinking, feeling, or acting. The answer tells me which world I'm functioning in. Good intentions and loving thoughts, for example, take place in the inner world but count for little or nothing unless acted out in the real world.

Then I began to study the character and functions of boundaries, especially personal boundaries. I learned that everything alive has boundaries. Without them, life on earth can not exist. Henry Cloud and John Townsend stress the importance of boundaries in their book *Boundaries, When To Say Yes, When to Say No To Take Control Of Your Life.* [1]

I found the condition of my personal boundaries to be chaotic. Important people were prevented from looking into my inner world — I was afraid of what they might see. On the other hand, dangerous and foolish ideas had ready access — I was afraid people wouldn't like me if I didn't agree with them. Additional items raced back and forth as if no border existed.

Most important, I learned that control of my boundaries is entirely my personal responsibility.

We All Have Boundaries

Every microscopic cell of every animal and plant in all the world is separated from its environment by a boundary, a wall, a membrane. Every form of life has a mortal dependence on its personal wall of life. The tiny, one-celled amoeba, visible only through a microscope, could not exist in its watery home if it were not for the membrane, the wall that separates the outside world from the amoeba's inside world.

This wall lets in exactly the right amount of fluid, no more and no less. It lets in nutrients, just the right kind and just the right amount. In addition, it lets out precisely the right amount and kind of wastes which otherwise would kill the organism.

Scientists speak of this kind of membrane as being "semipermeable." "Permeable" means things can get through; "semi-permeable" means only certain things can get through, and, more important, many substances which pass readily in one direction can not move back in the opposite direction.

Not all boundary walls are microscopic. Nations have walls, some as massive as the Great Wall of China or as notorious as the Berlin Wall. Others are just a line on a map. Boundaries serve to keep some people and certain items in and other people and items out. Houses have boundaries referred to as walls. The doors, windows, screens, locks, doorbells, peepholes, etc., serve to allow in or out only approved items and individuals at only approved times.

Some walls are less obvious than others. Each of us, for example, has a wall so obscure it can't be seen with a microscope, yet it determines precisely who we are, and it completely controls our relationships with the world.

This wall separates the physical world from the psychological world; it separates the world outside from the world inside. It separates what happens in reality from what happens in our minds. By doing so it totally controls our mental, emotional and spiritual sobriety.

Some of us have impenetrable walls.
People can't get in and we can't get out.
We are literally alone in a crowd.

Others of us have porous walls. We lack boundaries.
We indiscriminately let people walk in and "walk
all over us." In addition to letting them control our
feelings and our behavior, we repeatedly let them
abuse and take advantage of us.

We Do Have Control

My all-time favorite newspaper comic is
Calvin and Hobbs. Calvin is a six-year-old,
hyperactive boy who, in his mind, has his own
private, one-passenger space ship. When he feels
the need to get away, Calvin leaves the schoolroom
and travels to other planets and galaxies, passing
unscathed through meteorite storms, death rays,
intergalactic wars and related disturbances well out
of range of whatever is going on in school. Instead
of allowing his teacher or classmates to upset him,
Calvin closes the hatch and survives the school
hours happy and snug, alone in his tiny spaceship.

Aware or not, each of us is totally responsible for
the condition of our own spaceship. We and we alone
decide who and what gets in with us, who and what
is denied admission, and who and what is ejected.

Before recovery, on the assumption that it would make people like me, I let them into my ship by telling them the things about me I thought they would like, while keeping to myself the things I thought they would dislike. It didn't work. They didn't care for me and neither did I. I'd given away all the good and kept all the bad, and then wondered why I felt miserable.

Today I'm less likely to try to impress people with my accomplishments. Furthermore, there's nothing bad about me, that I am aware of, that isn't already known by at least one person in A.A. I've shared all that information with at least one person. As a result, it feels clean and pleasant in my spaceship.

Each of us is responsible for what passes in either direction through our boundaries. This includes those of us who, without realizing they have a choice, chronically complain that others make them feel badly.

A young man at our morning meeting, looking old for his age and squinting through the smoke from a cigarette burned down to almost nothing, said, "I have the impression people think of me as being very serious and very negative. They seem afraid to approach me because I'm always angry. That's not the way I really am deep down inside, but that's the way I act because I'm a reflection of what's going on in my life!"

Showing absolutely no awareness of being captain of his own spaceship, he described situations in his home which he insisted caused him to feel and act the way he did. He reminded me of me. I used to think, "You'd drink too if you had my wife (my life, my problems)."

We live simultaneously in two worlds: the outer, physical world, sometimes called the real world; and our secret, inner world, the world where God is, where we do our thinking, feel our feelings and establish our motives, attitudes and goals.

At one time I allowed events in the real world to largely determine how I felt, what I did and whether or not I drank. Today I am more "self-centered," centered in myself. With increasing frequency, all important decisions are made by me, and my life is devoted to keeping me comfortable inside in spite of whatever is happening or not happening outside.

Rudyard Kipling reflected this philosophy in his poem *If-* when he said, "If you can keep your head when all about you are losing theirs and blaming it on you . . . ." In a similar vein our Twelfth Tradition tells us to ". . . keep principles (internal world) before personalities (external world)."

My Area Of Responsibility

All my emotions reside in my inner world. And, whether I admit it or not, the extent to which they reflect the outside world is my choice. I need to think like Linus in the Peanuts comic strip who, when asked why he wasn't upset about the ridiculous things his older sister Lucy was doing, simply stated, "That's not my area of responsibility."

While responsible for little that happens in the real world, I am totally responsible for what goes on in my mind and for what gets in and out past the border between my inner and outer worlds. Other people have only as much influence in these matters as I give them. Viktor Frankl recorded perhaps the ultimate example of this when he described how the Nazis controlled in every conceivable way the destiny of the Jews, but were never able to control their attitude toward their destiny. Without the individual Jew's permission, the Nazis could not penetrate the boundary between that individual's inner and outer worlds.

I've gone so far with this concept of responsibility as to give Max a written Declaration of Independence. In it I accept total responsibility for my feelings. I can tell her I feel angry, but no longer can I say, "You made me angry." My feelings derive from me, not from her.

By the same reasoning, she is responsible for her feelings. When she feels badly, I can be understanding and supportive, but I don't have to feel responsible, and I don't always have to participate in her feelings. We were so enmeshed at one time in the past that a little voice in my head asked me, "Why don't we just be compassionate instead of getting upset every time she becomes irritable?"

Most important, my Declaration of Independence completely eliminates "emotional blackmail" as a manipulative technique. In past years the threat of taking a drink or of quitting meetings got Max's attention. Not any more. Al-Anon took care of that.

Incidentally, in my experience, alcoholics with an alcoholic spouse, relative, or friend can profit greatly by joining Al-Anon. But only as an Al-Anon member, not as an alcoholic. True, the Steps are the same, but the perspective is entirely different. In A.A., the primary focus is on alcohol; in Al-Anon, it's another person, an alcoholic. And other alcoholics give many of us alcoholics some of our biggest problems.

As for alcoholics attending Al-Anon meetings, in my opinion, it is inappropriate to announce at any Twelve Step meeting, whether it be A.A., N.A., C.A., O.A., Al-Anon or whatever, that one is a member of one of the other organizations. Such information is no more relevant to the purpose of the meeting than stating at an A.A. meeting that one is a compulsive overeater, sex addict, Al-Anon member, Catholic, Republican, doctor, priest or insurance salesman.

As far as the Declaration of Independence is concerned, I must admit it isn't as dangerous as it sounds. The contract is actually between me and the committee in my head. It helps me remember the line quoted earlier from The Twelve Steps and Twelve Traditions: "It is a spiritual axiom that every time we are disturbed, no matter what the cause, there is something wrong *with us*."

It also helps me to remember the words of the lady at an Al-Anon meeting years ago when she quoted Eleanor Roosevelt as having said, "No one can make you feel inferior without your consent." I remember thinking to myself, "Gee, if they can't make me feel inferior, they can't make me feel any emotion I don't want to have."

Psychologists and others who know about such things suggest that the first thing we should do when upset is to realize what is going on. We should say, for example, "I am upset." Then we should give ourselves permission to feel upset. Just because we are no longer newcomers and are sponsoring others doesn't mean we should never feel disturbed. It means we don't drink over our bad feelings. It also means that to the extent that we value our emotional sobriety, we don't sit around wallowing in the bad feelings for extended periods of time.

In addition to recognizing and giving ourselves permission to feel feelings, we should name them. Those of us who grew up in homes where the only feeling ever expressed was anger, must first learn the names of feelings. See Table 1 at the end of this chapter for a partial list. After giving the feeling a name, we are advised to discuss it with an appropriate listener such as a sponsor or one of our peers rather than with the committee in our head.

In my experience, having feelings, recognizing them ("I'm upset"), naming them ("I feel Angry!"), feeling them ("This feels awful!") and then talking openly about them, works. Denying feelings (pretending they don't exist) is about as effective as denying drinking — it doesn't work.

Taking Action

In addition to talking about our feelings, we can take constructive action regarding them. Anger, a form of focused attention and often the power behind destructive action, can be directed constructively. For example: the wife who gets so angry at her husband's drinking that she joins Al-Anon; or the TV actress mentioned in Chapter 1 who suffered from chronic lead poisoning and got so angry at her physicians that she discovered the cause of her problem herself. We often hear of alcoholics getting so angry at their sponsors for nagging them about the Fourth Step that they write it to prove it won't work, only to find it works as well as if they'd thought of it themselves.

An important psychological principle is that if we want to change the way we feel, we must first change the way we act.

To get over anger we have to talk it out and act it out — constructively. We turn our affective state, anger, into effective action.

Conversely, when we bury our feelings, we bury them alive. Bad feelings such as anger, like a fungus, survive in the dark and grow, while good feelings suffocate and die. On the other hand, good feelings like love and gratitude, when exposed to fresh air and sunlight, expand and grow while bad feelings shrivel and die.

"Be your own man," a father told his daughter in a recent TV commercial regarding the purchase of stock certificates. He insisted she purchase them herself rather than rely on a salesman. Be your own person he tells her. Take a leadership role in your own financial life.

Our recovery program tells us to take a leadership role in our emotional life. To be the person emotionally that we want to be, that God wants us to be, rather than the person circumstances and people want us to be. We give up the past and its ability to keep us in the victim role. We alone determine our emotional state. We can't afford to let others do it for us any more than we can let others decide whether or not we will drink.

As recovering persons we are what we think, feel and do. Others can't, without a gun, control our behavior. Likewise, unless we give them permission, they can't control our thinking or our feelings. To the extent that people (past or present, living or dead) have power over our feelings, it is power we have given them. And we can take that power back at any time. We aren't forced to take it back, but if we don't, we shouldn't whine about what they are "doing to us." By giving them the power, we have given them permission to do precisely what they are doing.

Progressing In Sobriety

E arlier, we established a working explanation of why alcoholics drink. We already knew from personal experience that Alcoholics Anonymous is a spiritual answer to that problem. And now that we've decided to stop letting others control our emotions, we should find it easy to enjoy long-term, comfortable sobriety.

Such would likely be the case if we didn't get involved in marriages and other close interpersonal relationships. These have destroyed many an otherwise powerful sobriety program. But such an outcome can be avoided by developing effective communication skills.

Read on. . . .

Table 1

How do you feel?

In case you don't know the language of feelings,
here are the names of a few.

abandoned	despised	indignant	shy
admired	determined	infuriated	sick
adored	detested	inhibited	smart
affectionate	disappointed	innocent	strong
afraid	discontented	inspired	surprised
aggressive	disgusted	interested	suspicious
alarmed	dissatisfied	jealous	sympathetic
alert	eager	jolly	tense
alienated	ecstatic	joyful	terrified
amazed	edgy	lethargic	threatened
amused	elated	liked	timid
angry	embarrassed	listless	tired
annoyed	enchanted	lonely	torn up
antagonistic	enraged	loved	trapped
anxious	enthusiastic	mad	troubled
apathetic	envious	mischievous	turned off
apologetic	estranged	miserable	turned on
appreciated	exasperated	mixed up	uncomfortable
apprehensive	excited	moody	undecided
approved of	exhausted	negative	unhappy
ashamed	fatigued	nervous	unimportant
at ease	fed up	obstinate	unloved
awed	forlorn	optimistic	unwanted
baffled	friendly	pained	unpopular
bashful	frightened	panicky	unsure
bewildered	frustrated	paranoid	upset
bitter	furious	passionate	useless
blissful	glad	peaceful	vengeful
bored	gloomy	pleased	vibrant
brave	gratified	popular	victimized
brilliant	guilty	proud	victorious
capable	happy	provoked	vigorous
cautious	hateful	puzzled	wanted
comfortable	helpless	regretful	weak
concerned	hopeful	rejected	weary
confused	hopeless	relaxed	wicked
content	horrified	relieved	wide awake
courageous	humiliated	reluctant	withdrawn
curious	hurt	resentful	worn out
cynical	hysterical	sad	worried
degraded	impatient	scared	worthless
dejected	important	seductive	wimpy
delighted	inadequate	serene	wretched
dependent	independent	sheepish	wrong
depressed	indifferent	shocked	

References:

1. Henry Cloud & John Townsend, *Boundaries, When To Say Yes, When to Say No To Take Control Of Your Life,* (Grand Rapids: Zondervan Publishing House, 1992).

For marital sobriety, I had to give up trying to change anyone but myself.

FOUR

INTERPERSONAL SOBRIETY
Communicating

Sober And Married

When asked why he'd spent the previous evening sitting in a bar watching his friends drink, the new A.A. member stated with obvious pride, "I wanted to test my sobriety."

Here's a better test: Stay married for over fifty years to the person you thought drove you to drink. If you manage that, take my word for it, you'll never drink again.

Divorces are common in our society, and from what I hear at meetings, they are often distressing and painful. Marriage, on the other hand, as Max and I can testify, isn't a constant state of bliss either.

Theoretically it could be. Alcoholism is a family disease. Everyone is affected, even the family dog.

Ideally, they all get into recovery. The alcoholic becomes a permanent, participating, enthusiastic member of Alcoholics Anonymous; the spouse a permanent, participating, enthusiastic member of Al-Anon; the kids participating, enthusiastic members of Alateen and later, Al-Anon; and the dog enthusiastically greets the many program people who visit the happy home. In this ideal situation, when the partner of the alcoholic is also an alcoholic they both become active members of both A.A. and Al-Anon.

The net effect is like having a podium in the living room. The home is governed by the Traditions, the individual members live by the Steps and slogans, and all agree, "Love and tolerance of others is our code." [1]

But even under these circumstances, marital sobriety can't exist without conflict. Physical sobriety follows automatically when we stop drinking. Mental sobriety evolves when we give up drinking and our old ways of thinking. Emotional sobriety begins after we give up drinking and our old attitudes toward people and problems. Marital sobriety, on the other hand, seems to require that we give up, not only drinking, but only God knows what else. As was heard at a meeting, "When I was drinking, all my spouse wanted was for me to stop drinking; now that I'm sober, there's no end to what's wanted!"

During the drinking years, Max wasn't all that easy to live with, and early in sobriety I thought "the courage to change the things we can" meant I'd have to choose between my marriage and my sobriety. Getting along well in interpersonal relationships has never been one of my outstanding characteristics. I've never been described as charismatic, and I have no explanation as to why I tend to get along least well with the people who are the most important in my life.

Sobriety is a growth process. I'm convinced that when we alcoholics hurt, we either drink or grow. If we don't drink, all pain becomes growing pain. In a marriage, when we survive a difficult situation without drinking, drugging or divorcing, we come out spiritually and emotionally stronger than we went in. As a couple, we grow together, or we grow apart. We don't stand still.

Max has always played an important role in my life, originally as a support, later as an excuse to drink, and more recently as an important adjunct to my total sobriety. Being as close to me as she is, she serves as a mirror in which I see and hear myself. In my reflection, I see who I really am. In this way, our combined lives, including our conflicts, have particular significance for me.

Life is a matter of priorities. Take drinking, for example. Either drink and enjoy it, or don't drink and enjoy sobriety. Don't alternate between drinking and not drinking. Don't give drinking and sobriety equal priority.

Marriage is similar. We ask ourselves what we are willing to give up to have the kind of relationship we want. Just as physical sobriety is easier to maintain if sobriety is more important than the right to drink, so marital sobriety is easier to maintain if harmony in the home is more important than the desire to convince the other person they are wrong and you are right.

Max and I don't think alike. I think vertically in that I pyramid a problem by narrowing it to a point and coming to a decision. She thinks horizontally in that she won't make a decision until she asks more questions. She wants more information; I want to condense what we already have. I like to express feelings; she doesn't. She likes to ask directions; I'd rather find it myself. She wants to do it later; I want it done now.

I like to keep it simple; she likes it complicated. I like things planned; she likes spontaneity. I answer a question directly; she answers by asking a question. I tend toward optimism, she toward pessimism. I think sequentially, in an organized manner. She thinks intuitively, in a random manner.

We don't even have that many interests in common. In the past, like many other couples, we ended our arguments with, "We probably never should have gotten married in the first place."

One of the most basic facts Max and I have discovered is that most of the time, although we differ greatly, neither of us is wrong. Odd as it may seem, we are both right. And, whether or not we should have married, we did.

Our job today is not to figure out if we should have gotten married, but to decide what we are going to do about it now that we are.

The following questions were presented at one of our communication workshops to help couples check their priorities in regard to their relationship:

1. To what extent do we work our Recovery Program in our home?
2. Which Steps control our relationship?
3. Which Traditions are practiced in our home?
4. Which slogans do we regularly apply to our relationship?

5. How do the Promises fit into our relationship? (Have we done the eight and one-half Steps that precede the Promises?)

6. Having taken the 3rd & 7th Steps, do we still criticize, condemn and complain throughout the day?

7. What part does Love play in our relationship, and what actions do we take to show it?

8. How does Powerlessness affect our relationship?

9. Is there "insanity" in our home?

10. Have I turned my will, life & spouse over to the care of God?

11. Do I have resentments toward my partner?

12. Do I have a sponsor and a working relationship with my sponsor?

13. Am I as aware of my shortcomings as I am of my partner's?

14. Which of my defects that interfere with a happy, comfortable relationship have I not yet asked God to remove?

15. Have I made a list of all persons in my home whom I've harmed and have I made amends to them all?

16. Do I take my own inventory and promptly admit it when wrong?

17. Do I treat my partner with the same love, tolerance and respect with which A.A. & Al-Anon members treat newcomers?

18. Do I have an adversarial relationship with my partner? Does either of us respond defensively to the other — or do we communicate as equals?

19. Am I a Victim or am I a Hero(ine) in our relationship?

20. Have we eliminated emotional blackmail from our home?

Max and I have worked hard on our relationship. Nowhere more intensely than in the area of communications. And nowhere have we needed more help.

We haven't turned to professionals to a significant degree. No doubt it would have speeded things up, but we chose to stay with our individual recovery programs and with whatever we could pick up on our own. We've read books, gone to communication workshops and talked to anyone willing to talk about getting along as a couple. Only a few of the many things we have tried are mentioned here. In general, we find these simple techniques much easier to do than to remember to do.

Even more difficult to consistently remember is that feelings are always valid. Whatever feelings either of us has at any particular moment, they are right for us at that time, and they don't have to make sense to anyone else.

In addition to the right to feel however we feel, each of us has the right to express our feelings. Expressing feelings honestly and in a manner that does not harm anyone else is known as being assertive. In general, nonassertive people are *passive, aggressive* or *passive/aggressive.* Passive/ aggressive people think, for example, "All right, I'll do it your way, but I won't enjoy it. And neither will you!" *Assertive* is none of these. Nothing has improved communication between Max and me more than learning to think and speak assertively.

Many community colleges offer courses in assertion training, and libraries and bookstores have a variety of cassettes and books on the subject. See the reference page at the end of this chapter for the names of a few. [2, 3, 4, 5]

Lately, when anticipating the satisfaction of a particularly passive/aggressive act I am about to commit, a little voice asks me, "Are we going to have to make amends for what we are about to do?" The fun is immediately gone. I hate knowing I'll have to come back later and make amends.

I feel miserable after a fight with Max, and I seem to be the one who always needs to make amends.

I've learned two important facts about amends: They're easier to make sooner than later, and they're easier to avoid than to make.

If I don't watch myself, I tend to make fun of Max in front of our friends. It's unfair and it lowers her self esteem. Furthermore, I've discovered that it's not possible for me to tear her self esteem down without tearing my own down too. In like manner, it's not possible to build up her self esteem without at the same time increasing my own.

I like me best when I behave neither passively nor aggressively; when I act neither defensively nor offensively; when I choose my behavior instead of passively reflecting Max's behavior.

To accomplish this, I make a conscious effort to remain emotionally independent of her emotional state. In addition, I remember that, not only do we each have the right to have feelings and to express them, but we also possess many other rights of which we may not be aware. And not being aware of rights is often the same as not *having* them.

Basic Rights

Here are a few examples of basic rights that belong to every one of us:

1. I don't have to give excuses for the things I feel, say and do.
2. I don't have to feel guilty just because someone else doesn't like what I do, think or feel. They are responsible for their own feelings.
3. I don't always have to be perfect and logical.
4. I don't always have to answer questions — not even my own.
5. I don't always have to be improving.
6. I don't have to be liked and admired by everyone in everything I do.
7. I don't have to spend the rest of my life trying to gain my parents' (or anyone else's) approval.
8. I don't always have to do what's best for me.
9. I don't always have to make sense.
10. I have a right to like myself and to say so.
11. I have a right to change my mind.
12. I have a right to like others and to say so.
13. I have a right to sometimes let others make decisions for me.
14. I have a right to not like, agree with, or approve of everything.
15. I have a right to accept or reject any information.
16. I have a right to my own opinion.
17. I have a right to be wrong.

18. I have a right to make mistakes and be responsible for them.
19. I have a right to be confused.
20. I have a right to relax and goof off sometimes.
21. I have a right to a lot more rights than just these!

Things go better when Max and I work on ourselves rather than on each other. Although it's painful and it seems unfair to have to work on one's self when the other person seems so obviously "wrong," the results are much more rewarding.

We've discovered that the more one partner in a relationship changes, the more difficult it is for the other partner to continue their old behavior.

Each of us has little control over the other's actions, considerably less control over their thinking, and little or no control over their emotions. Our only chance to change our partner's behavior is, with God's help, to change our own. As in tennis, if one partner stops hitting the ball back, the other soon stops playing tennis.

Max and I have declared our emotional independence of each other. She is no longer responsible for how I feel. I am no longer responsible for how she feels. I can no longer blame her for my feelings. She can no longer blame me for hers.

Of course it would be contrary to my recovery program for me to deliberately upset her. I'd have to make amends for that. But only I can decide when that is what I am doing. Besides, most of the time Max's Al-Anon program prevents me from controlling her feelings.

Emotional independence also prevents emotional blackmail. Formerly, when Max did things that upset me, I'd pout and treat her badly until she felt guilty and apologized for her behavior. Now, having declared our bilateral emotional independence, I can no longer get away with that — and neither can she.

During the drinking years I thought, *You'd drink too if you had my wife.* Now when I become upset, as mentioned earlier, a little voice asks, *Are you going to drink over this?* And when I respond, *Of course Not!* it asks, *Well, if you're not going to reward yourself with a drink, why do you get so upset?* . . . And I have nothing to say.

Max and I can't live together without annoying each other at times, but we can take turns. Whoever gets upset first, it's their turn. The other is obliged to remain calm until the storm passes. The worst, and yet the most common mistake either of us makes is to join the other in their upset state.

At other times we "draw a line." Have you ever had a heated discussion where no matter how hard you try and no matter what either one says, the situation gets progressively worse? When this happens, one of us will say, "Let's draw a line and start over." We continue to talk, but we keep moving forward. We don't rehash or repeat anything that's already been said. Some days all we do is draw lines, but that's better than fighting in circles.

In *That's Not What I Meant!*,[6] Deborah Tannen explains how parents teach their children to talk. Without thinking about it, they teach a conversational style. It's their own natural style, and there's nothing essentially wrong with it. But later in life it can be significantly different from the style of one's partner in a relationship.

Furthermore, in spite of the importance of this difference, it may not be apparent to either the participants or to a casual observer. They are more likely to think of themselves as intelligent people who simply need to talk their problems out. However, when their different conversational styles cause irritation and confusion, the more they talk, the worse the problem becomes. Outside help may be required.

Early in sobriety Max and I read John Powell's *Why Am I Afraid To Tell You Who I Am?*[7] Powell taught us the value of distinguishing different levels of interpersonal communications. We now think in terms of five levels:

1. **Cocktail Chit-Chat**
   The most superficial level. Important because conversations start here and move up."How are you?" "Fine." "Nice day." "What's up?"

2. **Talking About Others**
   "Have you seen Charlie?" "How's that fellow you were sponsoring?" "Did you know Jack was celebrating his birthday on Saturday?"

3. **Expressing Ideas, Judgments, Opinions**
   "I like the format of this meeting."
   "I liked what the speaker said about sponsorship."
   "People are sure friendly here."

4. **Expressing Feelings, Emotions, Attitudes**
   "I had the most delightful experience

today."
"I'm depressed."
"I need to talk to you about a resentment."

5. Peak Communications

The ultimate in intimacy. Those occasional, brief periods of complete and perfect communication between close friends or sex partners.

Even more important than learning about different conversational levels, we learned that feelings are neither "good" nor "bad." They have no moral value and should never be judged. The statement, "I'm uncomfortable around you," does not imply that you behave in an improper manner. Neither does it suggest there must be something wrong with one or the other of us. Instead it suggests, "There has probably been a misunderstanding. Let's talk."

Max and I know a couple whose marriage counselor told them, "Your marriage isn't working. I recommend a divorce." They left his office in silence. After lunch the husband said, "I don't know about you, but I'm going to that couple's communication workshop. You can come along if you want."

A year later at the same workshop and still married, they couldn't find the words to express their joy. They discovered that nothing was wrong with their relationship which couldn't be overcome by learning to communicate effectively.

Incidents of this type, plus our personal experience, convinced Max and me that if we wanted a happy and successful relationship, we would have to develop our interpersonal communication skills. We seemed to need more help in this area than just about anyone we knew. We needed it then, and we continue to need all the help we can get in communicating effectively.

In our search for help, we came across the work of two marriage counselors, David and Vera Mace, who practiced their profession together for fifty years. During the first twenty-five years, they worked with couples in trouble, couples breaking up because of problems such as money, sex, in-laws and children. During the second twenty-five years they founded what they called Marriage Enrichment, [8] an organization devoted to the improvement of good marriages. They discovered that these marriages survived the same problems (money, sex, in-laws, children) that created havoc in troubled relationships.

After years of study, the Mace's came to the conclusion that healthy marriages had three distinct features that were lacking in troubled marriages. Essentially, these were:

1. *A commitment to the spiritual and emotional growth of one's partner;*
2. *A commitment to learn and to practice communication skills;*
3. *A commitment to resolving conflicts creatively.*

When I first read this, I thought, *What an order!* But then I began to see the similarities to the A.A. and Al-Anon programs. When both partners in a relationship go to one or both programs and encourage the rest of the family to do the same, they demonstrate their commitment to each other's emotional and spiritual growth.

As for learning communication skills, where would A.A. and Al-Anon be without communication, without the caring and sharing that activate the meetings? And where better to practice these skills than at home?

The third item, creative problem solving, becomes a necessity when, as stated in the Big Book of Alcoholics Anonymous, *". . . we have stopped fighting anybody or anything."* [9] It is impossible for two people to live in essentially the same space without generating conflict, and when fighting is no longer an option, we are forced to find alternatives. We stop our old behavior, and experiment with new approaches. We become creative.

Not fighting doesn't mean the "silent treatment." It means dealing with conflicts in a non-adversarial way without reacting either defensively or offensively. Each time Max and I give up one of these high-energy techniques that don't work and funnel our energy into a more effective approach, we find the changed behavior less difficult than anticipated.

What could be better in sobriety than two people living together and committing themselves on a daily basis to their partner's spiritual and emotional growth, learning and practicing communication skills, solving conflicts creatively and building their partner's self esteem by making them feel important?

Our treatment of each other is reflected back to us. When Max and I first met, she smiled at me. That inflated my ego, and I smiled back at her. Every time I paid attention to her, she felt better about herself, and every time she paid attention to me, I felt better about myself. We raised each other's self-esteem.

During the drinking years, because I disliked myself, I said things that hurt Max and lowered her self-esteem. She responded by saying things that hurt me and lowered my self-esteem. This became habitual, and we were bad for each other. Today, like most couples, we are either good or bad for each other depending on the messages we send.

I can think of nothing more important in a relationship than the support of a partner's self-esteem. One sure way to accomplish this is to make them feel important. My favorite definition of love is, "making the other person feel important." And, since we can make people feel important by trying to communicate with them, every effort to do so, whether "successful" or not, is an act of love.

Someone once said, "A measure of communication is the result it produces." In other words, if you don't like what happens when you communicate with your partner, change what you are doing. I have found that the more I change my behavior — the way I communicate — the more Max and the situation change.

Communicating In A Relationship

Interpersonal relationships consist of two multifaceted personalities exposing to each other different facets of themselves while they continually change as they grow in recovery. Such a complex dance cannot proceed without communication. When two people are together, there is

---

no such thing as "no communication." Refusing to speak is communication. The sex act is communication.

Every relationship is an exercise in communication. Indeed, life consists of relationships (among people, places, things, situations and combinations thereof), and of communications with and about those relationships. As such, life is a continuous communication problem.

Here is a list and a brief discussion of some of the communication techniques we've heard about over the years. They've certainly improved communications in our house.

Here's a relationship quiz: You and your partner have not been getting along well lately. Suddenly you are accused in a loud and angry voice of something you didn't do. Do you react, or do you respond?

Professional counselors make an important distinction between these two activities. The first implies an immediate answer; the second connotes an interval of time (hopefully for thoughtful consideration) before replying. The knee-jerk reaction of practicing alcoholics when confronted with a problem is to immediately become angry and drink. In recovery, although alcoholics give up drinking, they don't always give up reacting instantly in an unthinking and destructive manner.

Reacting

Here are a few of the reactions some of us have tried:

Completely forget the Steps, Slogans, Big Book and recovery.
Instead, focus exclusively on the problem.

Mirror the other person's abusive behavior.
Insist they are making us act the way we are acting.

Insist on controlling the other person's behavior and mood.
Of course, this puts us completely under that person's control. What we do next depends entirely on whether or not they do what we want.

Continue to punish the other person even when we want to make up.
They haven't suffered enough yet. Don't tell them what's wrong, or what we want, or what we are thinking. If

they loved us, they'd know. They'd be able to read our minds, the same way we read theirs.

Develop a long list of "should's" and "ought's."
"I should...; she should...; we ought..."

Obsess on, "If only...," and "What if...."
"If only I hadn't said that."
"What would have happened if...?

Demand to know "Why?"
Refuse to be consoled until someone explains to our complete satisfaction why reality is the way it is.

Fight.
Do this either overtly (aggressively) or covertly (passive/aggressively).

Pout.
"I feel miserable, and everyone else should feel miserable too!"

Escape into health.
"I'm just fine. You're the one that's crazy."

Get angry.
> Kick the dog. Yell at the kids.
> Punish. Become defiant. Run away.
> Sleep somewhere else. Refuse to talk.

Play the martyr.
> Assume a passive role. Submit.
> Acquiesce. Comply. Be the victim.
> Have an anxiety attack.

Plan your suicide.
> "I'll show you, I'll kill me!"

We could increase the list ad infinitum.

A number of professionals have suggested names for some of the negative ways of reacting in a communication situation. Here are examples.

Self Justifying.
> This is extremely common in relationships and results from a desire to "win." It consists of each person hearing the voice and the words but not the message of the other, and then restating what they, themselves (rather than their partner), have already said. It sounds like this:
> He, "Yackety, yackety, yackety."
> She, "Chatter, chatter, chatter."

He, "What I said was, `Yackety, yackety, yackety.'"
She, "And what I said was, `Chatter, chatter, chatter.'"
He, "But can't you see that I'm saying, `Yackety, yackety, yackety?'"
She, "So!! Well, why won't you admit that I'm saying, `Chatter, chatter, chatter?'"
He, "How can you be so damn stupid?"
She, "My Gawd! *You're* the one that's *Stupid!*"

Defensiveness.

This causes a great deal of difficulty between couples. In recovery, since we've admitted that our lives have become unmanageble, our best defense is often our defenselessness. In Al-Anon we hear, "Don't complain and don't explain." Especially don't ever explain your feelings. You feel the way you feel because that's the way you feel. No one said feelings have to be logical, and you don't need anyone's permission to feel them.

Defensiveness is often a sign of insecurity. One night I returned to a meeting I'd helped start in a hospital where I worked. It was a happy occasion. A former patient was excited about introducing me to his new, non-alcoholic, non-Al-Anon wife. When I jokingly commented on his increase in weight, he playfully said, "It's her fault!" He meant it as a compliment, but she began to chastise and harass him, demanding, "If I fixed (blah, blah, blah), would you (blah, blah, blah) anyway?!!!" She was angry, he was embarrassed, and the whole episode turned sour, all because of unnecessary defensiveness.

Talking Over.
Starting to talk before the other has finished speaking. Many families, especially in certain cultures, talk this way all the time. It's their style, their manner of carrying on a conversation. Under these circumstances there's nothing wrong with it. But to an uninitiated, unsuspecting partner in a relationship not raised to communicate in this manner, it can be confusing, intimidating and infuriating. In addition, the cause of the problem may not be apparent to either partner.

"Yeah-butting."
This often precedes Talking Over and is commonly heard at meetings when the newcomer responds to

everything said with, "Yeah, but...".

Mind Reading.
The equivalent of, "Yes, that's what
you said, but I know what you meant."

Winnie E., one of my favorite Al-Anon speakers,
used to say she played a game with her husband
called "Guess What I'm Thinking." According to
Winnie, her husband told her she could walk into a
room, ask a question, answer it, walk out and be
mad. That's mind reading!

Cross-complaining.
A form of defensiveness. When your
partner complains about you,
complain about her. Anytime she
mentions anything she doesn't like
about you, tell her things you don't
like about her. This snowballs and
results in a non-conversation or worse.

Kitchen Sinking.
Cross-complaining at its best. Throw
in every rotten thing you can think of
except the kitchen sink.

Catastrophizing.
Gross exaggeration of the absolutely
horrendous, insurmountable, cat-
astrophic outcome if things don't

turn out the way you think they should.

I Win, You Lose.

Making winning more important than being loving. Or wanting the other to lose even if you, yourself can't win. Since your partner is not your enemy and the problem is only a challenge, stick to being loving. That way you both win, both grow, and nobody loses.

Getting Off The Beam.

You both lose sight of what the conversation was about. Everything said makes the situation worse and a fight is developing. Stop talking. Agree to "draw a line" and start over from a new base without repeating anything already said. Teamwork of this sort solves problems.

Rudeness.

Treating your wife like "a wife," or your husband like "a husband." Instead, treat your mate like a secret lover. We have different styles of speaking in different relationships under different circumstances. Ask yourself if your current style is appropriate and is it getting you what you want.

Responding

By not reacting, by simply avoiding these impediments to effective communication, your conversational skills will improve, and hopefully your partner will begin to change. To further improve the situation, you might respond with empathy. All good listeners practice empathy.

When your partner expresses emotions, thoughts or feelings, no matter how bizarre, do your best to understand and possibly to share those emotions, thoughts or feelings. Empathy is the ability to say to one's self, If I were this person in precisely this same situation, I'd feel exactly as he or she does.

To actually feel another's feelings to the point of suffering along with them is sympathy. Sympathy is what the pre-Al-Anon, "codependent" mother or father feels when their alcoholic gets into trouble, and they suffer as much as, or more than, the alcoholic does. Sympathy is exhausting; it leads to so-called "burnout." Empathy is energizing; it leads to harmony.

Here are a few ways to show your spouse that you empathize with his or her feelings and opinions.

Validation.

Validate by convincing your spouse that you are able to see things from their perspective and through their eyes. That is, if you had been born of their parents in their place and had all their life experiences, thoughts and assumptions, then you too would think and feel exactly the way they do.

Validation is an extremely important aspect of good communication.

You are not saying you agree with them. You are saying you understand where their feelings and opinions may be coming from even though you don't necessarily share them. It's a matter of walking in the other person's moccasins for a moment, and the best way to demonstrate this is by giving feedback.

Feedback.

This is an excellent technique for preventing resentments. After listening carefully, respond by saying, "What I heard you say was. . . ." You'll be surprised how often what you heard is not what your partner meant. The misunderstanding becomes apparent when you paraphrase.

Paraphrasing.
This involves repeating in your own words what you thought you heard your partner say. Clarifying meanings at this point eliminates a great deal of argument later. Someone once gave me a desk sign that read, "I know you believe you understand what you think I said, but I'm not sure you realize that what you heard is not what I meant."

In paraphrasing, be sure to cover both aspects of what you think you heard your partner say.

Include both the facts (description of the incident as they saw it) and the feelings (how they apparently felt about it).

Of the two, feelings are the more important. However, they may have been expressed only non-verbally in such things as speed, volume or tone of voice, choice of words or facial expression. In other words, your spouse may not actually tell you how they feel. It's up to you to figure it out from the way they act.

Remember, you don't have to agree with what was said. You merely say in your own words what you think you heard and how you think he or she feels about it. If your spouse disagrees with your interpretation, do not argue. Calmly ask for a clarification. Do not express your own opinions or feelings at this time, and do not ask them to defend what they said or how they felt.

For example, after hearing your spouse describe a particularly trying day, you might say, "It sounds like you've had a bad day."

As in a game of charades, the key words are,
   "Sounds like. . . ."
   "Sounds like you're angry."
   "Sounds like you're depressed."
   "Sounds like. . . (whatever emotion is evident)."

Professional listeners use this technique when a client becomes angry at them. Since fighting with a client isn't practical, they say something like, "Thank you for that information. I'll process it later." An Al-Anon lady I know says to her husband when he's angry at her, "Thank you for loving me enough to tell me how you feel." These are examples of validation by means of paraphrased feedback.

A Communication Formula

There's a world of difference between saying, "You made me angry," and, "I am angry." The first is an accusation. It claims that they are responsible for the way you feel. That's not possible.

No one can make anyone else feel any particular emotion. We don't have that much power over each other.

Caring about another's feelings without feeling responsible for them makes for pleasant communications. Even more satisfying is the ability to express one's own feelings without having to defend them.

Here's a formula for doing this:

"I feel _____ "
(state how you FEEL, not what you THINK)

"when you do what you did _____(when)_____ "
(don't be judgmental or sarcastic)

"in such & such a situation _____ "
(give a precise time and place)

For example:

"I feel embarrassed, put-down and unimportant when you talk over what I am saying and change the subject before I have finished speaking like you did when we were with Bill and Jean last night."

When the other person's behavior has a direct effect on your life, you can include that fact. Here's how George expressed himself to his spouse:

"I feel frustrated and angry when you ignore our budget and go on a spree like you did yesterday, buying clothes and stuff we agreed not to buy. Now I can't pay this month's bills."

The formula becomes:

"I feel _____ when you do what you did _(in such & such a situation)_ because _____"

In the beginning, you might try writing the statement out in order to say it correctly. Having read or stated it, do not argue. You have not made an accusation. Nothing needs to be defended. Remember, you have a right to have feelings and to express them. Indeed, in a relationship this amounts to an "obligation" as well as a "right."

Responding By Reframing

Professionals trained in dealing with client problems utilize a technique called "reframing." Anyone can do it. Simply change the point of view. Just as a picture looks different in a different frame, so too a situation looks different when viewed from a different perspective. For example, seeing the drinking of an alcoholic as a sign of weakness evokes a picture quite unlike that created by viewing it as a symptom of a disease.

A person will often reframe their own problem when what they have said in describing their problem is repeated back to them in the words of the listener. Apparently, people in the middle of a problem don't hear what they're saying about their situation until it is repeated by someone else. Someone has said a problem well-stated is a problem half-solved. They also said a problem shared is a problem halved.

Reframing takes place when we change our thinking from, "I'm not going to put up with this anymore!" to, "I can handle this one day at a time." It can be as simple as remembering, "Life by the yard is hard; by the inch it's a cinch," or, "We choke on life by the loaf, but thrive on twenty-four-hour slices." Our A.A. and Al-Anon slogans work by reframing our thinking. They get us to look at situations differently.

I sometimes reframe problems that arise from the treatment I receive from others by telling myself that people treat me the way I have taught them to treat me. This takes me out of the victim role and gives me a choice. If, by my past behavior, I have shown people that I will tolerate their offensive behavior, then I have the option of changing their behavior by first changing mine.

Reframing is what sponsors do, and what sharing is all about. Other reasons may exist, but essentially we share problems for one of three reasons: we need to talk them to death, we want sympathy, or we want a solution.

In the first instance, all we need is someone to listen. In the second, we won't hear or appreciate a solution if it's offered. In the third instance, we need someone to show us the problem in a different light, a different frame, a frame that gives us different options as to what we can do.

People who refuse to share their problems, in the mistaken belief that sharing is whining, are indulging in self-pity. My problems, they think, are so bad I could never share them.

At the request of a friend, I once talked to a depressed A.A. oldtimer. He'd married a woman who insisted she didn't need a recovery program because she had her church. As a couple, they had problems, but he couldn't talk to her about them. He refused to share at the Alano Club that he visited daily because, he insisted, "It would be bad for the newcomers." Instead, after twenty-five years of not drinking, he killed himself.

Reframing includes giving up the idea of being trapped (we always have options), or of being a victim. Someone has said there are no victims, only volunteers. It also provides the opportunity to sometimes give a particularly vexing problem the so-called "short version of the Serenity Prayer" ("To H___ with it!").

Reframe By Changing

Whom To Change?

Most people seeking help from a marriage counselor want to know how to get their partner to change. The A.A. and Al-Anon programs, and specifically the Steps, on the other hand, focus entirely on changing ourselves. Even the Serenity Prayer tells us that after we've changed everything we can, we should change our attitude by accepting whatever is left.

What To Change?

We often hear at meetings, "If you keep doing what you're doing, you'll keep getting what you're getting." Dramatic results often follow when we simply stop doing what isn't working — drinking and fighting, for example.

All sorts of possible changes could be suggested.

Recognize your resentment or it may kill you.

Pray for the other person instead of assuming the role of victim. The Big Book suggests night and morning on one's knees as the best time and place for prayer.

Stop mirroring your opponent's behavior.
Let them copy yours. Don't mimic the other person's shouting, swearing or abusive behavior. Be the person you and your Higher Power want you to be.

Stop insisting the other person change.
Be the first to change. Set an example. Be a "program of attraction."

Stop putting energy into the problem.
An A.A. Winner (Clancy I.) says he allows interpersonal problems to solve themselves by holding on to the thought that whoever gets drunk first loses.

Leave and be comfortable or stay and be comfortable.
Leaving to get comfortable may be a geographic. Staying and whining about it is boring. Let comfort be your goal.

Write a letter to God explaining all the facts.
I always feel better when I know that God knows what's going on down here because I've told Him the whole story in writing.

Give up all notions of how it should be handled.
If you hold on to any idea how God should handle a situation, you haven't turned it over

Exercise and play.
Putting energy into the problem keeps it alive. Take care of yourself instead. Put your energy into the answer.

Reframe By Asking Questions

Max often reframes a problem by asking herself three questions:
"Is it important?"
"Is it any of my business?"
"Is there anything I can do about it?"

Her answers determine what she does next, if anything.

Other reframing questions might include:

"Which Step applies to this situation?"
I have never failed to find an answer to my (or anyone else's) problem in one or more of the Steps.

"What do the Traditions say about this?"
Many families function beautifully by adhering to the Traditions in all their affairs.

"What is the loving thing to do?"
My partnership with God includes the agreement that if I do a thing for the right motive and leave the results entirely up to Him, everything will turn out precisely the way it is supposed to (and love is always a right motive).

"Is the other person doing the best he or she can?"
I have come to the conclusion that I have done the best I could every day of my life up to and including today, and so has everyone else. If I (we) could have done better, I (we) would have done better. If this is true, the other person is doing the best they can at this moment.

It also helps if I tell myself: If I had been born in this person's body with their hereditary pattern, and had lived every minute of their life up to this moment, I would act exactly the way they are acting now.

"What does God want me to do?"
I tried for years to get God to help me.
He never did. Eventually I recognized
His willingness to let me help Him do
His will, but His total disinclination to
help me do mine.

"What would an A.A. Winner do?"
When we alcoholics hurt, we either drink
or grow, and if we don't drink, all pain
becomes growing pain. In this way we
become A.A. Winners. (Some days I grow
more than I want to.)

"What does the Big Book say?"
It says plenty, and the bottom of page 86
and top of 87 tell us precisely what to do
when faced with a problem.

"What do I want from my partner?"
Make a list. Write down five things (common courtesy, for example) that you want
from your partner. Now, give those five
things to him or her.

What other reframing questions might you ask?

Progressing In Sobriety

So, suppose you do the do's and avoid the don'ts, but your spouse isn't interested, won't try these techniques and would rather pout or argue. What then?

Try writing notes and letters. Writing eliminates those impulsive, dangerous, "mouth-in-motion-before-brain-in-gear" reactions that can be so detrimental to a relationship. In a sense, a letter expressing honest feelings, even feelings of anger, is a love letter.

Leave your note or letter in a place where it will be found. Don't expect a reply. Be content that you expressed your feelings without defending yourself and without an argument. A response may come later, maybe much later and maybe only after many letters.

Remember, the conflicts in our relationships provide opportunities for our growth as individuals. If we change, our partner will probably change. If not, at least one of us will have grown.

Remember, merely attempting to communicate, particularly when it is difficult, is an act of love.

And love is never wasted. We can't love one person more, without loving everyone, including ourselves, a bit more. In like manner, we can't resent anyone without resenting everyone including ourselves a bit more. We get back what we put out. We reap what we sow.

That is a spiritual axiom, and it brings us to the matter of spiritual sobriety which is the subject of the next chapter.

References:

1. *Alcoholics Anonymous*, 3rd ed., (New York City: Alcoholics Anonymous World Services, Inc., 1976), p. 84.

2. Herbert Fensterheim & Jean Baer, *Don't Say Yes When You Want To Say No*, (New York: Dell Publishing: 1975).

3. Jean Baer, *How To Be An Assertive (Not Aggressive) Woman . . . In Life, In Love & On The Job*, (New York: Rawson/ Macmillan, 1976).

4. Manual J. Smith, *When I Say No I Feel Guilty*, (New York: Bantam Books, Bantam ed., 1975).

5. Robert E. Alberti & Michael L. Emmons, 4th ed., *Your Perfect Right*, (San Luis Obispo, CA: Impact Publishers, 1982).

6. Deborah Tannen, *That's Not WhatI Meant!* (New York: Ballantine Books, 1986).

7. John Powell, *Why Am I Afraid To Tell You Who I Am?* (Niles, IL: Argus Communications, 1969).

0. David R. Mace, *Close Companions, The Marriage Enrichment Handbook*, (New York: Continuum Publishing Co., 1987).

9. *Alcoholics Anonymous*, 3rd ed. (New York: Alcoholics Anonymous World Services, Inc., 1976), p. 103.

For spiritual sobriety, I had to give up feeling Guilty!

FIVE

SPIRITUAL SOBRIETY
Feeling Guilty!

Controlled By Guilt

In the beginning, religion (as distinct from spirituality) came easily for me. I had no uncertainty about God or His plans for you, for me or for anyone else. In time though, doubts began to creep in. Over the next forty years, I compensated for my increasing uncertainty with increasing religious fanaticism. When no longer able to stand the strain, and before my church could expel me, I discarded it. Unaware that I had any other choice, I threw God out too. As my spiritually happy friend Marion S. told me later, "Paul, you threw the baby out with the bath water!"

An unknown number of years later, right after New Year's Day 1967, without warning and

against my better judgment, I found myself in an
A.A. meeting.

They were laughing. They laughed at all sorts of
embarrassing things — even their drinking. After
seven months of meetings, I found myself laughing
with them — I haven't had a drink since.

However, gut-level laughter didn't blend well
with my lifelong guilt. I was born guilty,
guilty of a heinous crime committed many years
before I was born, by a couple of people I didn't
even know.

As I understand the story, even though God knew
the first man and his girlfriend would do what
He told them not to do if He told them not to do it,
He told them not to do it anyway. And when they
did what He knew they'd do, He acted surprised,
and He demolished the Garden of Eden. To this
day, no one has been able to determine its original
location.

Not only that, God stayed angry. Then He insisted
that people feel guilty for having upset Him. He
sent down plagues, famines, fires, tempests and
pillars of salt in an ongoing effort to control the
people He said He loved. I felt like a certain weary
Jewish gentleman who, I understand, on being
informed that, as a Jew, he was "one of God's

chosen people," wondered aloud if God couldn't perhaps choose someone else for awhile.

This congenital guilt was only the start for me. Later came guilt for things I did, things I failed to do and things I thought about doing while still too young to do them.

Thinking it, they insisted, was as bad as doing it. Well, in my limited experience, it certainly wasn't as much fun, and therefore the penalty ought not be the same. I've since wondered if the twisted logic of that ruling of the church had anything to do with the late President and proclaimed Catholic John F. Kennedy's statement, "Life is unfair!"

I misunderstood the basic function of guilt. I thought it had great spiritual value in that God loved us the most when we felt the most guilty, and enough guilt compensated for all sins and made us spiritually healthy.

In addition to the common forms of guilt, I suffered from that special brand reserved for heretics and agnostics — those who entertain doubts about the teachings of the Church. Today I realize I probably misunderstood those teachings. Besides, the teachers were talking about their Higher Power, not mine.

All my early authority figures, including my parents, used guilt as a control technique. Any time they disapproved, they resorted to anger, retaliation, intimidation and punishment. I observed, learned and perfected their techniques. When things didn't go my way, I made an open display of my displeasure so the people responsible would feel guilty for having upset me. If they didn't notice, I turned up the volume.

In children this is called pouting; in adults, sulking, but it needs a more descriptive name.

Manipulated by guilt myself, I used guilt to manipulate and control others. Knowing no other option, I continued this passive/aggressive behavior for many years in spite of the unhappy, guilt-ridden interpersonal relationships it generated.

Importance Of Faultfinding

Guilt can't survive without blame. In order to know who to blame, I had to find fault. I excelled at faultfinding. Never was I unable to find the other person's defect, error, mistake or fault. Faultfinding became my shield, my protection, my approach to life. Knowing who was at fault, I knew who to blame. And who to make feel guilty.

According to Brian Tracy, [1] blaming is the garden in which negative emotions grow like weeds. Tracy claims that a list of all the negative emotions totals fifty-four. Furthermore, he insists that every one of the fifty-four can be completely eliminated from anyone's life. All anyone need do, according to Tracy, is completely and permanently eliminate all faultfinding and blaming from their lives.

Maybe so. I wouldn't know.

Old ideas die hard. I thought God liked humility and that humility meant groveling: telling God I was worthless, sinful, derived from dust, meaningless, insignificant and trivial. I told Him I felt unworthy to even try to communicate with anyone as omnipotent, omnipresent, omniscient, kind, wonderful and loving as He.

I didn't really believe the stuff I told Him, but I hoped He would. . . . He didn't.

In the movie "Amadeus," about the life of Amadeus Mozart, I identified with Salyerie, the villain. All Salyerie wanted out of life was for God to make him a famous and successful musician and composer. Instead, God gave all the fame to that odd, little fellow, Mozart. At the height of his anger at God, Salyerie tried to kill himself ("I'll show you, I'll kill me"), and he ended his days in an insane asylum.

My story is similar. I never liked the inconvenience of long-distance travel, but in my mind I agreed to fly to Norway or wherever to receive the Nobel Prize in Medicine for discovering the cure for, say, cancer, high blood pressure, the common cold, or something like that. Of course, I first needed God to give me the answer, but when they gave me the Nobel Prize, I'd give God all the credit. I was going to make God famous. He had merely to make me famous first. I thought it quite a bargain. But, He never bought it. Instead of making me famous, He made me anonymous.

Prior to becoming anonymous, I groveled and begged, "Help me! Help me! For God's sake, God, help me!" God didn't answer. He didn't even listen. So, we parted company.

Now, in sobriety, my working relationship with God is, in a sense, the same. He still refuses to help me by working for me, by doing my will, by helping me run my life my way. On the other hand, He's quite happy to let me help Him.

I can help Him do His Will, but He won't help me do mine. On my will, I work alone.

A friend, asking if I wanted to hear a riddle, inquired, "How do you make God laugh?" Answer: "Tell Him your plans."

Speaking of laughter, there seems to be a connection between spirituality and humor. Early in sobriety, not only did my A.A. group, with its laughter and sense of joy, keep me sober, it prompted the rekindling of earlier spiritual feelings and, in a sense, the group became my Higher Power.

A.A. members live by the old Chinese beatitude, "Blessed are they who can laugh at themselves; they shall never cease to be entertained." AA's laugh at things they take seriously. They laugh, for example, not at God, but at their weird ideas about God and religion and guilt. Mary R., always serious about sobriety but light-hearted about life, says, "It wasn't the apple on the tree that caused all the trouble. It was the pair on the ground."

A.A. Stands For Altered Attitudes

When someone said, "A.A. stands for Altered Attitudes," I set my goal at finding a new set of attitudes. "Rule 62: Don't take yourself too damn seriously," [2] became my motto and my personalized license plate.

Later, when hopelessly lost in a rainstorm while looking for a particular A.A. meeting in Palos Verdes, I noticed a "Screw Guilt" bumper sticker

on the car in front of me. Identifying with that
sentiment, I instinctively followed the car. We
stopped directly in front of the meeting hall.

Spiritual peace began to evolve at a more rapid
pace after Jim, an ordained minister working in
the chemical dependency field, provided an
important insight. Hearing about my lifelong,
pervasive sense of guilt, Jim informed me that
clergymen know from experience that every body
of people, on being exposed to the teachings of
religion, automatically divides itself into two
groups: those who find a Loving God, and those
who find a Punishing God. "You," he said, "chose
the latter."

What a relief! Shared guilt weighs less than
solitary guilt. I was no longer alone, no longer
unique. Others made the same mistake, the same
dumb choice. Others tormented themselves with
warped ideas about God.

In addition, having evicted the former tenant, I
now had a spiritual vacancy, a place in which to
build an entirely new spiritual belief system up
to and including my own personal version of a
Higher Power.

About this time I heard Bob C., a wise old-timer,
say, "When we do the Steps properly, the past loses

its power to harm us." I interpreted this to mean
that A.A. really is *The Land of Beginning Again.*[3]
It gave me a fresh start completely free of guilt
and emotional suffocation. The Big Book expresses
a similar idea when it says, "We will not regret
the past nor wish to shut the door on it," and ". . .
in God's hands, the dark past is the greatest
possession you have. . . ."[4]

None of these statements had immediate validity
for me. Raised with the lifelong admonitions, "Let
your conscience be your guide," and "If you feel
guilty you are guilty," I still had a strong sense of
guilt even after completing all twelve of the Steps.

But then I wondered: If guilt feelings are as
beneficial as claimed, why aren't we all mentally
and spiritually a whole lot healthier than we are?

> *Eventually I decided to focus on the
> distinction between being guilty and
> feeling guilty.*

Being funny isn't the same as having a sense of
humor, and being guilty isn't the same as having
a sense of guilt. Examples abound of guilty
criminals on one hand who feel no guilt, and of
innocent people on the other hand who suffer from
an outrageous sense of guilt. This latter condition
is known as scrupulosity.

Dealing With Defects Of Character

The inability to experience guilt, as manifested in the psychiatric condition known as antisocial personality disorder, is a serious defect of character. I decided that my excessive and debilitating sense of guilt was also a defect of character. Then, instead of working on it as a guilt problem as advised by my earlier teachers, I decided to treat it as a defect of character. I gave it to my Higher Power to handle via the Sixth and Seventh Steps. [5]

I told Him I'd like to be completely and totally rid of my excessive sense of guilt. But I understood that things like this were sometimes useful to Him or to my fellows, so would He take all of it for tonight, sleep on it, and in the morning give me back precisely the amount He wanted me to have. I agreed to accept whatever He returned to me as a personal gift from Him.

Since then I've made God the same offer concerning other defects such as anger and fear. Then I decided that in my case insomnia and depression were defects of character. Certainly they were having a negative effect on my personality, and I had made no progress in treating them as illnesses or as a so-called, "chemical imbalance." So I also offered them to God.

Of the many times I've offered a defect to God in this manner, He has never responded by immediately removing it completely. Neither has He ever failed to remove a sizable segment of it. Furthermore, the remainder continually decreases in intensity as I become progressively more friendly with it.

> *Trying to obliterate defects by putting energy into them, by fighting them and by hating myself for having them only made them worse.*

On the other hand, total acceptance of myself, Rule 62, and becoming friendly with my defects neutralizes most of their power. Referring to defects as demons, someone who knows about such things, said, "Hug your demon; otherwise it'll bite you in the ass."

Establishing A New Belief System

In *The Art Of Hanging Loose In An Uptight World*,[6] Ken Olson points out how as children during our formative years we unwittingly accept the values and goals of the people who raise us. This occurs so naturally that we don't realize we have other choices.

I had acquired my beliefs regarding God, religion, right and wrong, politics, prejudice, guilt and much more in this manner. Then sobriety gave me the opportunity to install my own goals, values and beliefs. The right to do so had always been there.

I began to establish my current belief system by accepting as true the first 164 pages of the Big Book. [7]

> *I decided to base my life on the assumption that if it's in the Big Book, it's true as far as I'm concerned. This eliminated massive amounts of doubt and uncertainty.*

I also chose to accept the statement in the back part of the book saying that nothing happens in God's world by mistake. Although unprovable either way, some people like to argue this concept. Personally, I choose to believe God knows what He's doing and what's going on down here. How can anyone have confidence in a God who might at any moment exclaim: "Oh, My Gawd! Look what I just did. I pushed the wrong button! Look down there; have you ever seen such a mess?"

God and life are complicated beyond my ability to understand. I accept that fact, and I no longer sit and drink while thinking about imponderables.

What can't be explained, I leave alone. Life is a problem only if I make it a problem. When the time comes for me to understand why Evil exists in a world created by a Loving God, I'm sure the answer will appear.

Not only do I not know why Evil exists, no one else knows either. I recall many years ago on a Sunday morning being at a retreat which centered around the problems of sin and evil. Near the end of the weekend, during a lull in the question and answer period, I asked the retreat master, a priest, "Since God is all-knowing and therefore knew in advance precisely how this whole thing was going to turn out, why did He create it anyway?" The priest hesitated a moment, looked me in the eye and moved on to the next question.

Until knowledge replaces my ignorance, I prefer to not accept the explanations commonly offered for the existence of Evil. The story that Adam and Eve caused all the suffering in the world by eating an apple from the Tree of Knowledge doesn't satisfy me. Neither does the idea that someone as powerful, or even more powerful, than God, someone called the Devil caused it. These stories don't appeal to me. God being a God of Love, where the devil did the Devil come from? If Hell exists, who built it? Who issued the building permit? Certainly not *my* Higher Power!

If Hell was created by Satan — allegedly one of the original Archangels who had a serious falling out with God — that would mean one of God's top executives, one with enough power and influence to create Hell, couldn't establish a satisfactory relationship with Him while living with Him. Yet you expect me, a weak, fallible human being to do it while living down here. That's asking too much. I'd rather not believe that story.

Many people are willing to accept any plausible explanation, especially when offered by an authority figure, rather than admit they don't know. Max, my wife, often tries to win arguments with me using that ploy. When I reject an explanation she's dreamed up, she asks, "Well then, what's your explanation?" When I admit I don't have one, she claims her explanation must therefore be correct.

I don't find it difficult to say, "I don't know." And I'd rather make up my own explanation than accept someone else's just because it's popular.

Scientists do this all the time. Ed Regis [8] wrote a book about the Institute for Advanced Studies, the scientists who live there and the problems they think about. Scientists create theories to explain the things they don't understand. They use the theory as long as it works and discard it when it no longer fits the facts.

For example: Scientists can't find the outer limit of space. They know it's more than 10 billion light years away and receding in all directions at the speed of light. Neither do they know the size of the smallest atomic particle, but they believe it to be less than 10 to the power of minus 291 centimeters. They use the Theory of General Relativity to explain everything in outer space, and the Theory of Quantum Mechanics to explain everything inside the atom. However, the two theories are not compatible with each other.

Now someone has come along with the theory of "superstrings," and they refer to it as the Theory of Everything. It explains things both large and small. If it works out, the two older theories will be discarded.

Progressing In Sobriety

I figure, if they can do it, I can do it. If many of the explanations of life are just theory, and those theories don't help me stay comfortably sober, then I might as well dream up my own. That's what I've done, not to change anyone else's mind or convince anyone of anything, but simply to keep me well ahead of the disease which is following me. I call this my spiritual calisthenics, my spiritual aerobics. I'll share some examples in the next chapter.

References:

1. Brian Tracy, *The Psychology of Achievement,* Audiotape Series (Chicago: Nightingale-Conant Corp.)

2. Alcoholics Anonymous World Services, Inc., *Twelve Steps and Twelve Traditions,* (New York City: The A.A. Grapevine, Inc. and by Alcoholics Anonymous Publishing, Inc. [now known as Alchololics Anonymous World Services, Inc.]), p. 153.

3. "The Land of Beginning Again" appears in *Best Loved Poems of the American People,* selected by Hazel Felleman (New York City: Doubleday, 1936). It refers to a place where all our past grief and mistakes can be laid aside and never picked up again.

4. Alcoholics Anonymous World Services, Inc., *Alcoholics Anonymous*, 3rd ed. (New York City: Alcoholics Anonymous World Services, Inc., 1976) pp. 83 & 124.

5. ibid., p. 76. Step 6: "Were entirely ready to have God remove these defects of character." Step 7: "Humbly asked Him to remove our shortcomings."

6. Ken Olson, *The Art Of Hanging Loose In An Uptight World,* (Prescott, AZ: O'Sullivan Woodside & Co., 1974).

7. Alcoholics Anonymous World Services, Inc., *Alcoholics Anonymous*, 3rd ed. (New York City: Alcoholics Anonymous World Services, Inc., 1976)

8. Ed Regis, *Who Got Einstein's Office?* (Redding, MA: Addison-Wesley Publishing Co., 1987).

*For further spiritual sobriety, I had to give up
my old belief system.*

SIX

SPIRITUAL AEROBICS
Fantasizing

Spiritual Fantasies

The Big Book has a chapter to the agnostic — those who believe we can not know for sure whether or not God exists. But it ignores those of us who know He exists but discarded Him when we discarded the religion of our childhood. If God lives in a church, how does one find Him when there is no church?

What is church and religion anyway? What's the difference between living a religion and living a spiritual way of life such as found in Alcoholics Anonymous? As someone in A.A. said, religion is for people who want to stay out of Hell; spirituality is for people who've already been there.

My friend Don S. says, "Religion takes place between God and me in association with people in the community; spirituality takes place between God and me inside my head."

Being religious and being spiritual are not the same. One can be either, neither, or both. Many A.A. members make religion a supplement to their recovery program. Others make A.A. a supplement to their religion. And many find God outside of religion.

Not only are there hundreds of religions with various descriptions of God, there are semi-religious belief systems which specifically exclude God. Atheistic communism, for example, replaced God with "The State." Atheistic psychoanalysis replaces the concept of god with Freud's concepts. And many psychologists and psychiatrists believe in the power of the subconscious mind. They talk to it, send affirmative messages to it and beseech it for help with problems — all in a manner resembling prayer and meditation.

Could God be fooling these men of science by hiding in the last place they'd think to look, inside themselves, inside their own minds?

That's where I found God, inside my head in the Center of Calm in the center of me. And, as mentioned earlier, finding God inside my head allowed me to make peace, first with Him and then with the personalities in my head. Now, I'm generally able to distinguish between His voice and theirs.

A believer believes in God; an agnostic believes we can't know for sure; and an atheist believes there is no God. Frankly, I think atheists take God much too seriously. They develop an image of God and then spend the rest of their lives trying to prove such an entity doesn't exist.

If an athiest is one who doesn't believe in God, what do you call someone who doesn't believe in the Devil? That's what I am. I've cast the Devil out of my life.

Oddly enough, when I did that, my Higher Power underwent a personality change. He no longer has a dual personality. He's a God of Love now with no interest in score-keeping and punishment. Today we are the best of friends.

My Higher Power thinks we waste too much time and energy trying to figure out whether or not He exists. It's not an arguable matter. All arguments in favor of His existence are completely countered by the arguments against His existence.

Viktor Frankl [1] believes the existence of God is as natural as water. "Nature wouldn't give us thirst" says Frankl, "if It hadn't given us water to quench it, and Nature wouldn't have given man since the beginning of time a thirst for God and the Ultimate Meaning of Life if there were no God, and Life had no meaning."

Meanwhile, I'm sure of this:

> *A life based on the belief that God exists and is our friend is far superior to a life without that foundation. And this would be true even if God did not exist!*

Our problem is not one of proving we're in the Palm of His Hand; our problem is to act as if that were true and to stop acting as if it were not true. Action is the key word here.

Suppose someone gave you a book of blank checks and told you, "There's a million dollars in the account. Write checks, and you can have the money." Would you write them? Or would you say, "That's too good to be true," and not write any checks? If so, you'd be right: if you wrote no checks, there'd be no money for you.

These days, I write plenty of checks on my spiritual bank account. I also write code letters like "CCC" in the palm of my hand to remind me that I'm in the palm of His Hand and that I should   act accordingly.

Every day, via the Third and Seventh Step prayers, I turn over to God everything that happens that day in both my inside and outside worlds. By doing this I feel that I give up my right to Criticize, Condemn or Complain about anything or anybody for the rest of that day. This doesn't work perfectly, but it definitely helps me stay centered in me rather than in "them." And the committee in my head certainly appreciates the much narrower focus.

Today my Higher Power fills the role of good friend plus what might be called Supersponsor. Certainly He works some sort of program, and of course anyone in His position would have to remain anonymous. With all His alcoholic children, He couldn't get by without adhering to at least some of the Al-Anon principles. I know from personal experience that He follows the Al-Anon practice of allowing alcoholics the dignity of taking the consequences of their own behavior.

My real-life sponsor, Jack, and I have a rather unusual relationship in that we sponsor each other and have done so since our first few months in sobriety. While not the usual relationship, it works for us.

My Relationship With God

The first time I took the Third Step, I took it with Jack as my witness. Then I decided to repeat the Third Step Prayer before each of my three Home Groups. I did this on the theory that more witnesses would make it impossible for me to change my mind. I'd have to get all those people together to rescind my decision about letting God have charge of my life.

My comfort level rose appreciably as soon as I put God in charge. However, the source of most of my work problems, the telephone, still caused me considerable concern, especially at night. To correct this, in my mind I rerouted all telephone calls through my Higher Power's switchboard. From then on I knew no call could get through to me without first being screened and approved by Him. Knowing this I relaxed and found my work far easier and much more enjoyable.

As my working relationship with God continued to improve, I decided to set up a Limited Partnership with Him as the General Partner and me as the Limited Partner. I gave Him a 51% controlling interest in my life, and to make the decision binding on both of us, I filled out a Limited Partnership Agreement obtained at a business supply store. To complete the deal, we wrote out the Terms of the Agreement, a statement of responsibilities of each partner.

We now have it in writing that He is in charge of worry and I am in charge of work. And He doesn't like me to help Him with the worry, and He never does any of the work.

Also, according to our contract, I don't sit and do nothing while waiting for Him to tell me what to do. I tried that once. I decided to not move in any direction until He told me what would happen if I did this, as opposed to what would happen if I did that. After a lengthy period of waiting, I realized He was quite willing to let me sit there and starve before He'd give me that kind of information. I am not permitted to see into the future.

I can do anything I want. I can do it with a great deal of planning or none at all. I can try very hard or just a little. Either way I must leave the outcome up to Him. Whatever happens as a result of anything I do or fail to do is strictly His responsibility. My job is to look at my motive, then do what's in front of me. The outcome is none of my business. Whatever follows is God's Will.

It is specifically against my contractual agreement with God for me to plan, plot or scheme to control the consequences of my actions. I can only ask myself, "What's my motive?" If my main motive (I usually have more than one) is right (love is always a right motive) and I leave the results up to Him, things turn out the way they're supposed to.

Creation hasn't stopped. The Bible says God created the world and everything in it in six days and on the seventh day He rested. It fails to mention that on the eighth day He went back to work and has been working day and night ever since — Sundays and holidays included.

The net effect of my partnership arrangement with God is that He and I are now co-creators of my day. I determine my attitude; He determines reality and the outcome of my actions. Together these determine the kind of day I have.

In all humility, most days my contribution seems the more significant. As mentioned earlier, it's hard to have a bad day with a good attitude, and it's hard to have a good day with a bad attitude.

No Mistakes

Do things ever happen by mistake? A fellow I sponsor returned from a men's retreat saying the retreat director disagreed with the statement in the Big Book that nothing happens in God's world by mistake. As mentioned earlier, many share that opinion, but I'd rather believe God is never surprised and never makes "mistakes."

Nothing is unforeseen by God. Not because He has predetermined it (God is more all-knowing than all-controlling), but because He has always known that everything would be precisely the way it is right now. Every pebble, every blade of grass is where it has been known through all eternity that it would be at this precise moment.

There is no past or future in God's world, only this present moment. Time is an invention of man in his attempt to make sense of the Big Picture. God knows only the eternal Now.

> *When we mind-trip into the past or into the future, we travel alone. God stays in reality, in the Now.*

There never will be a time when a voice will boom out of the sky proclaiming, "Your attention, please! This is The End of Time, the beginning of Eternity! Turn in your watches, clocks and calendars. From this moment on, Time stands still!"

Nor will Judgment Day be predicted. CNN won't forewarn us. The Evening News won't provide a countdown like they do on New Year's Eve. We're already in eternity and everything fits. The Big Picture makes sense, but we don't understand it because we can't see enough of it. We can't see enough in either time or space.

Possibly we never will. Then again, we might. Our confusion derives from our narrow perspective, our tunnel vision. Very likely, from a different perspective, in God's time, and when we are no longer concerned about it, we'll suddenly realize: "Oh, that's why things were that way back then!"

Like looking at a news magazine with a map showing a small area and another map showing the general location of the smaller area, the large-area map makes the small-area map understandable.

In the beginning, according to the Bible, there was nothing but God. Then God created us. Out of what? Presumably out of Himself. We must have been created out of some sort of God-substance. This validates my belief that God resides deep within each of us, and in so doing, determines in large measure our essence, our humanity, our personality, indeed, who we are.

And since God resides within each of us
equally, we all presumably have the same
spiritual potential, the same germ of
creativity, the same potential for joy,
humor and laughter.

Created in His image and likeness (whatever that means), we are manifestations of His handiwork and He wants us to enjoy His creation. I know my Higher Power wishes we'd spend less time complaining, belittling and finding fault with ourselves. He'd prefer that we cultivate a healthy sense of self-importance, self-confidence, self-approval, and especially self-acceptance. He'd like us to enjoy being who we are.

He'd also like us to develop the same loving attitude toward our spouses, our children and every alcoholic and non-alcoholic with whom we come in contact.

Prayer And Meditation

Prayer and meditation was the topic for discussion at our morning meeting recently. The room seemed full of gurus who'd spent years perfecting meditation techniques. Prior to sobriety I'd specialized in prayer and mediCation. In sobriety I decided to learn to meditate the way we're supposed to. Using techniques I learned from books, lectures, demonstrations and audio tapes, I can reach heights of spiritual ecstasy lasting anywhere from twenty to thirty seconds. Then one of the personalities in my head yells, "Hey! Why is everyone so quiet? What's going on?"

I shush him. I stress the importance of absolute silence. I tell him we're going to meditate like this for twenty minutes twice every day from now on. This really gets him going. "You've got to be kidding! There's too much happening out there! This is one more example of your self-centered-ness. Let me out of here!"

His shouting wakes all the other personalities in my head. They get excited. Chaos results.

On the other hand, I meditate often and effectively when engaged in other activities such as when trying to get to sleep, when jogging or walking the dogs, or when in the car alone with the radio off. Other times include sitting in meetings, waiting in line or going into or returning from a problem situation. In short, on all sorts of occasions. These periods of spontaneous spirituality have become a habit, and with each repetition they become more effective.

I've also developed a better way to deal with problems. Instead of merely thinking about them, I do automatic writing on my computer. Originally I used a pen, then a typewriter, and now my computer. Starting with "Dear God," and giving no thought to what I am going to say, I write to my Higher Power about a problem or situation. I don't stop to read my writing, to think about what I am saying, or to correct punctuation or grammar. No one is going to read it anyway.

The more often I do this, the more productive it becomes. Answers appear out of nowhere before I finish the letter. If not, they pop into my mind later that day or upon awakening the next morning or during the following day when I'm thinking about something else. The Big Book refers to this as intuitive thinking. God talks to me via intuitive thoughts, answers, and ideas. He's the source of whatever creativity, humor and love I possess.

Fantasies

I choose to believe God exists, is my friend and wants to see me happy.

That simple idea works well for me. It adds a strong, positive direction to my life, and if, as some people say, it is only a myth, then I might as well make up more fantasies to make me comfortable.

Tired of wondering why you're an alcoholic?

I was never meant to be an alcoholic, and it bothered me until I figured out how it happened.

Where people are made, one assembly line turns out drinkers; the other turns out non-drinkers. Near the end of the drinkers' line there's a little old man named Joe. He's been standing there all through eternity counting from 1 to 10 and stamping every 10th drinker "Alcoholic." He's tired, bored and irritable. Just as I came by, someone yelled, "Hey, Joe!" Joe half-turned and yelled, "What do you want???" As he did so, he stamped me — by mistake. I was supposed to be a "9".

How to explain the fact that Max and I have been around now more than seventy years and married over fifty?

Our files have been lost Up There. If they aren't found, we'll be here forever.

What's the meaning of Life?

God created everything that exists, including all our memories. He created everything we know about history plus all the scientific evidence that the world has been here for billions of years. He created it all in a flash just fifteen minutes ago. He created it for no other reason than to see how we'd react.

Wonder about the battle between God and the Devil?

It's over. God won and the Devil has capitulated. Hell no longer exists. What do we do now?

You're standing at The Pearly Gate seeking admission.

St. Peter asks, "While you were down there, what was your predominant mood, attitude, or emotion?"

You suspect he wants to hear "Guilty!" but you're not sure. Instead of answering, you ask why he wants to know about your attitude rather than your sins. He puts his hand gently on your shoulder and says, "I'll tell you why. We've given you all sorts of opportunities to learn the art of joyful living. If you haven't learned it down there, you aren't going to learn it up here."

He continues to explain. "As you know, this is a place of happiness, peace and joy. What you don't know is the secret of how we keep it that way. We don't admit whiners, complainers, or unhappy, resentful people. We figure if they didn't like it down there, they aren't going to like it up here either, so we let them go to another place. That's Our reason. Now, what's your answer?"

Here's one of my favorite fantasies:

Physicians and other authorities can't agree on the cause of alcoholism.

This leaves me free to have my own theory. Until proven otherwise, I choose to believe alcoholics and other chemically-dependent individuals, whether they want to or not, generate a great deal of love, but lack the ability to express love. This causes pressure which builds up like the pressure in a tea kettle. Alcohol and drugs relieve the problem temporarily but worsen the communications problem. The situation gets progressively worse.

Not only can alcoholics not give love, they can't accept love. As a result, the spouse, relatives and friends who love the alcoholic can't express their love either. They develop many of the same symptoms as the alcoholic.

The pressure of unexpressed love continues to build up on both sides of the relationship. Eventually it forces its way out as frustration, resentment, anger and other negative emotions, including hostility and violence. As a result, the communications problem continues to worsen.

Doctors, lawyers, clergymen, none can help. There's nothing anyone can do. Eventually the alcoholic comes to A.A., and the spouse, relative or friend comes to Al-Anon.

What do we do with these newcomers? We love the hell out of them. We love the hell out of their hellish lives. We treat them with courtesy and respect. We care about them. We share with them. We make them feel important. We love them. The alcoholic stays sober and the spouse begins to recover. They don't even know what's happening to them.

Soon, following our example, they give someone newer than themselves a cup of coffee, a smile, a place to sit, a handshake, whatever it takes to make them feel important. They have begun to act lovingly without realizing what they are doing.

We don't call this Love. We call it Action. Love is Action, the kind of action modeled at Twelve-Step meetings.

As you can see, I have the right to believe anything that seems plausible to me. We all have that right. Look at the work of Freud. He came up with all sorts of unprovable explanations. Today psychoanalysts and many psychiatrists continue to believe what he said simply because he said it and because no one has come up with a more compelling explanation.

Progressing In Sobriety

Sometimes an explanation seems obvious. For example, alcoholics obviously drink because they want to and could stop if they *really* tried.

But being obvious doesn't make an observation true. If it did, the world would be flat and the sun would rotate around the earth.

Believing what I was told because it was obvious and because it was the only explanation available didn't keep me sober or comfortable.

Sobriety followed when I stopped trying to think my way through life and took the actions recommended and modeled by sober alcoholics.

Continuing those actions and modeling them for others has kept me sober. And accepting everything in the Big Book as true, while adding

personal, workable, but unprovable fantasies has
kept me both sober and comfortable.

I intend to go on using that combination as long
as it continues to move me forward in my quest
for total recovery.

References:

1. Viktor Frankl, *Evolution of Psychotherapy, A
   Conference Infomedix*, (Garden Grove, CA:
   Milton H. Erickson Foundation, Inc., Dec.
   1990) Oral communication.

*For continuing, comfortable sobriety, I had to
learn that acceptance is not approval, it's a
challenge!*

SEVEN

SPIRITUAL PHILOSOPHY
Accepting

Sobriety Diamond

Father Barney used to come to our area from Seattle to put on retreats for A.A. and Al-Anon members. He had a way of breaking sobriety into its different aspects by comparing it to a baseball diamond. He said first base was physical sobriety; second base, mental sobriety; third base, emotional sobriety; and home plate was spiritual sobriety.

I liked that concept but wondered how I got to first base without spiritual help. Then someone pointed out that one can't get to first base without starting at home plate.

As I see it, we come to Step One soon after passing first base, and Step Two is located just this side of second base. The rest of the Steps are encountered as we run for third and head for home.

Some people get to first base and try to steal the rest of the bases. The really lucky ones get another chance at bat.

We can't stand still on this diamond. If we aren't progressing in spirituality, we are drifting slowly or rapidly back toward a drink.

The Serenity Prayer

> *God, grant me the serenity to accept the things I cannot change, courage to change the things I can, and the wisdom to know the difference.* [1]

In our search for increasing spirituality, the Serenity Prayer plays an important role. Our meetings often open or close with it. Who wrote it, and how did it acquire such importance?

According to one story, in 1926 Reinhold Niebuhr, the famous writer/lecturer, as a guest, gave the sermon at an Easter Sunday service. As he walked home, a friend asked how he might obtain a copy of the prayer Niebuhr had read. Instead of copyrighting the prayer, Niebuhr reached in his pocket and handed it to his friend.

In time, greeting card companies printed it. It spread to servicemen overseas; then all over the world. In 1942 it reached the New York office of A.A. via the obituary column of a New York newspaper. [2]

Bill W. said that when he and others in the office saw the prayer, they felt it expressed the basic sentiment of A.A. so well that they had it printed on little cards. For several years they included one in each mailing that went out to the various groups. He said, ". . .with amazing speed the Serenity Prayer came into general use and took its place alongside our two other favorites, the Lord's Prayer and the Prayer of St. Francis." [3]

Every morning, and repeatedly throughout the day, I recite the Third and Seventh Step prayers along with the Serenity Prayer. The Serenity Prayer tells us precisely how to deal with any problem.

The Serenity Prayer asks God for gifts. It mentions serenity, acceptance, change, courage and wisdom. According to Webster, wisdom is "a wise plan or course of action," [4] and that is what the prayer

gives us. The power word is "change." The prayer
offers us only two options: *either change the
situation or change your attitude toward it.*

Nothing more? What about bitching, whining,
pouting, sniveling, sulking, complaining, griping,
ranting, shouting, quitting, fighting and all the
other aggressive and passive/aggressive activities
which seem more appropriate? Don't they count
for anything? Besides, how do we know what to
change and what to accept?

Father Barney used to say that 99.44% of what
we have to accept is out there, and (tapping his
chest) 99.44% of what we have to change is in here.
Still, it seems almost immoral to accept things
without a fight, and it's hard to know when to
stop fighting.

Courage

Change requires courage. The familiar, even
when painful, offers a sense of security in
contrast to the fear of the unknown. Recovery
involves change and change involves risk.

It takes courage to come to A.A.. Thousands, if
not millions, of alcoholics would literally rather
die drunk than join Alcoholics Anonymous.

It takes courage to speak at a meeting, to lead or read at a meeting. It takes courage, more than some of us have, to write a Fourth Step and risk someone finding it. It takes courage to read it to someone and risk being disliked or laughed at, or having our secrets revealed to others.

It also takes courage to ask to be sponsored. It takes courage to agree to be a sponsor. It takes courage to live the A.A. program. It takes courage to live out there, totally sober, in a drinking society. And it takes a great deal of courage to accept life on life's terms.

My first thought when facing conflict or risk is to run, to escape from the problem. The truth is however that all my problems, whether in my head, in my marriage or out there in the real world, have collectively provided the necessary stimulus to every bit of progress I have made in finding out who I am and who God wants me to be.

No journey of discovery could be more exciting. Yet, although I am not aware of any significant growth on my part in the absence of conflict, my choice has always been a life completely free of tension and stress. If I had had my way, I would have missed everything that is important to me in my life today.

Change

My mind is like a powerful searchlight. It highlights and intensifies whatever it looks at, and it prefers to focus on causes rather than solutions. When I'm upset, I want the person or situation causing the difficulty changed. Since I am right, they must be wrong. Go after the cause. Keep the focus out there where it belongs.

Quite a few years went by in my sobriety before I fully appreciated an Al-Anon member's statement that the more we try to control another person, the more we are under that person's control. Neither of my two major life problems (alcoholism and people) responded to my attempts to control them. Instead, they controlled me.

My alcoholism resulted from the conflict between my mind insisting I could drink and my body insisting I couldn't. The fundamental cause of the problem lay hidden in my genes which I could not change. I could change only my attitude. I haven't had a drink since I accepted that fact.

The same with people. Max, the person closest and most readily available, became the focus of my people problem. I told myself I couldn't leave her because I'd feel guilty for walking out. In truth, I was too dependent on her to leave.

I took the next choice. I set out to change her. Most of the years we've been married I have tried, with varying degrees of intensity, to change Max. I've consistently done this in spite of the fact that I don't have a shred of evidence that it ever has or ever will work. Indeed, I can't recall a single instance of any person in my life ever having changed because I convinced them I would like them better if they did.

I remember my surprise many years ago reading in a book on child training that people never change as a result of being told they ought to change. They only change, the book said, when they feel totally accepted as they are.[5] Only then does it feel safe to change.

Not until well into recovery did I become aware of an additional option. I could change my attitude. I could accept that which was bothering me. But how could I do that when I didn't approve of what needed to be accepted?

Approval

I've always considered it appropriate to either approve or disapprove of every person, place, thing and situation in my life. However, the Serenity Prayer, which places great emphasis on acceptance, doesn't even mention approval. The reason: we live in two worlds. In God's world, approval has nothing to do with acceptance.

In the real world it does. If you don't like merchandise, don't buy it. If purchased and unsatisfactory, take it back. In assertion training class they tell you, don't be obnoxious but don't be a wimp either. Don't accept merchandise and service that doesn't meet with your approval.

> *In the spiritual world, the psychological world, the world between our ears, the only world where happiness can be found, approval isn't even a consideration.*

I can't imagine one of God's messengers rushing up to God saying, "We've got a big problem, God. Paul doesn't like the day we sent him." I get a picture of God thinking of another place I can go if I don't like the way He's running things.

Approval, a requirement for acceptance in the outer world, is actually an impediment to acceptance in the inner world. Life doesn't seek our approval. It insists we accept life on its terms, and doesn't care whether or not we approve.

Our challenge is to be emotionally comfortable regardless. Situations often change after we accept them. They never change simply because we're unhappy.

Acceptance

At an A.A. meeting I once quoted another A.A. member as having said, "Life is not painful; it's our resistance to life that is painful." Afterward, a young woman strongly disagreed. She said her thirteen year old son had had a motorcycle accident while drinking. "He'll be a paraplegic for the rest of his life. I certainly can't accept that!"

We talked awhile about the difference between acceptance and approval. Some time later, she looked like an entirely different person. She had accepted the challenge life offered her and had turned her massive resentment from destructive anger into constructive action.

Attitudes being contagious, her son had adopted her new approach to life, and they were both busy sharing, caring and working with other paraplegics. Typical of the A.A. way of life, they had turned a strong negative into a strong positive. They moved from victim to hero, from living in the problem to living in the answer. They picked up the challenge of paraplegia the way A.A. members pick up the challenge of alcoholism.

Acceptance has at least two deficiencies: it has no duration, and it's not transferable. I often hear people say, "I turn my will and life over to God in the morning, but take it back as soon as I get to work."

I doubt if that's literally true. They didn't change their mind about accepting God's will. Instead, the acceptance they felt so sincerely in the morning applied only to life at that moment. Life then exercised its right to change the situation without notice. The situation giving them trouble now is not what they accepted in the morning. Acceptance doesn't carry over. It has to be repeated over and over and over again with every new situation and circumstance.

Acceptance isn't a destination; it's a continuous process, a journey, a philosophy, a way of life. Failure to recognize this can result in all sorts of problems including a return to drinking. Once we accept our powerlessness over alcohol, we ask for help and we get sober. After a period of time, some of us forget to continually renew our acceptance of our powerlessness, and we end up drinking again.

Acceptance isn't predetermination, passivity, quitting, or acquiescing. It's the opposite. It's picking up the lance and facing life's challenges bravely.

It's being a hero, not a victim; active, not passive; winner, not whiner. Acceptance is getting on with life, not sitting back whining, complaining, blaming, resenting, justifying or faultfinding. It's not all those things that seem so natural and normal, but which only make matters worse for one's self and for everyone else.

It also seems quite normal to ask the question "Why?" Like approval, "why" is more than appropriate in the material world, but it is definitely an impediment to acceptance and to emotional sobriety. I once heard Rev. Robert Schuller on TV express the opinion that when people ask God "Why," they don't want an explanation, they want an argument.

What's the difference between acceptance and surrender? As I see it, surrender comes first. We give up. We stop doing whatever we've been doing that isn't working. Then we relax. (*Easy does it. Let go and let God.*) While relaxing, we look around to see what we can do to make a success of our lives in spite of the current circumstances. We decide to change our attitude to one of acceptance.

Acceptance isn't a closed fist angrily holding onto what it wants. It's an open hand that has dropped what it was holding and is now ready to receive whatever life has to offer.

Doctor Viktor Frankl, the Jewish psychiatrist mentioned earlier who survived the Nazi concentration camps, in talking about the ultimate meaning of suffering, speculated that the highest level a person can achieve in life is to survive with dignity and courage a difficult fate . . . and then to teach others how to do it.

"When terrible suffering is borne with dignity and courage," he said, "when you take your cross upon yourself with courage, you not only squeeze out the meaning to such a terrible event, but you reach even the highest possible level of meaning."

Upon hearing this statement, I thought how appropriately it could be applied to the members of Alcoholics Anonymous and the other Anonymous programs. During my first seven months in A.A., and even though I didn't really believe it, I admitted I was an alcoholic. Then, on July 31, 1967, I accepted the fact that, even though I had no choice in the matter, I was, perhaps as a result of a cosmic mistake, a mild sort of alcoholic.

At that moment my life changed dramatically, and it has gotten progressively better ever since. If my life were pictured on a graph stretching from left to right, the curve would be downhill, my life deteriorating until the day I accepted my alcoholism. Not a straight line down. There were ups and downs with enough ups to keep me from recognizing the chronic downward trend.

The curve would continue its up and down swings but with a pronounced upward slant beginning immediately after my sobriety date and continuing until today and presumably on into the future.

For me, both alcoholism and sobriety have been progressive conditions, alcoholism progressively downward, sobriety progressively upward.

What happened on my sobriety date to cause such a momentous change? What did I actually accept when I accepted my alcoholism? Apparently I accepted the challenge of living life successfully in spite of the fact that I can't drink like other people. As a result, on that date I moved from living in the problem to living in the answer. I moved from the role of victim to the role of hero in my own life's story. I moved from a life of hopeless inactivity to a life with more to do than I can possibly accomplish in one lifetime. I moved from whiner to winner. Above all, I moved from being just another drunk, to being a sober member of Alcoholics Anonymous.

At every moment of every day, life asks each one of us, "Which role do you want to play in your life story today? The play goes on regardless, but you have a choice. Do you wish to be the Victim or the Hero? The choice is yours."

Progressing In Sobriety

As I see it, the graph of my life will continue upward as long as I continue to do the things that have brought me this far.

I want all I can get of this way of life, and I'm limited only by how long I can stay here. Therefore, I'm going to stay around as long as I can, and with ever-increasing enthusiasm, I'm going to continue to do everything that has been working for me.

References:

1. Bill W., *The Language of the Heart*, (New York: The AA Grapevine, Inc., 1989.), p. 269.

2. (Luckily only the first stanza. The rest tends toward sin and guilt, the sort of thing many of us have too much of already.)

3. A Co-Founder, *Alcoholics Anonymous Comes of Age*, (New York: Harper & Brothers, 1957), p. 196.

4. Victoria Neufeldt and David B. Guralnik, *Webster's New World Dictionary*, 3rd ed (Cleveland: 1988), p.1533.
   (On the other hand, Webster's equates serenity with tranquillity. They are not the same. Tranquillity is a cheap imitation of serenity. Tranquillity comes in either a liquor bottle or a prescription bottle, while serenity can't be bottled. Forest Lawn epitomizes tranquillity. Serenity, rather than the absence of a tempest, suggests calmness in the presence of turmoil. To paraphrase the quote of Rudyard Kipling mentioned earlier, *serenity is keeping your head when all about you are losing theirs—and blaming it on you.*)

5. Thomas Gordon, *P.E.T., Parent Effectiveness Training*, (New York: Peter H. Wyden, 1973), p. 31.

For chemical sobriety, I had to give up mind-affecting prescription drugs.

MEDICATING SAFELY
Medicating

My Point Of View

When I was four years old, my father purchased a house drug store combination, and I grew up in an atmosphere of "Better living through chemistry." This environment said no matter what's wrong with you, there's something you can buy that will make you well or will make you not care that you aren't getting well.

To further my knowledge along these lines I went to pharmacy school and medical school and then specialized in Internal Medicine. For twenty-eight years I practiced medicine as a certified diagnostician with special emphasis on the use of prescription medications to treat the medical problems of adult men and women.

At the height of my career, after being forced against my better judgment to attend meetings of Alcoholics Anonymous, I recognized my addiction to both alcohol and my own medications. Not only had I missed the diagnosis, so had a neurologist, five psychiatrists, a medical social worker, and several priests. Even the Mayo Clinic didn't know what was wrong with me until Max, my wife, betrayed me by telling them about my nocturnal drinking and pill-taking.

Now, after closely associating with and treating alcoholics for over twenty-five years, I have certain opinions regarding the relative safety of mind- and mood-affecting medications. These I share as opinions, not as advice. I have no opinion on the newer antidepressants and tranquilizers which came along after I left practice and which are said to be nonhabituating, but I recall hearing the same thing about the old ones when they first came on the market.

All through my medical career and now in A.A., I repeatedly hear people say that alcoholism results from an inability to handle life's emotional problems. In retrospect, I wonder if I didn't first learn the real cause of alcoholism back in the 1930's in pharmacy school.

At that time, one of my favorite books was Goodman and Gilman's textbook of pharmacology and therapeutics.[1] I don't recall the year of publication, but under "Diseases Caused by Alcohol," the authors listed a medical condition called Pathologic Reaction to Alcohol. They described this as a disease wherein the patient displays grossly abnormal, unusual and inappropriate behavior after the ingestion of only a relatively small amount of alcohol. They said the condition was "uncommon." But today I wonder, could doctors Goodman and Gilman, without realizing it, have been describing the root cause of alcoholism?

Still today, the American Psychiatric Association [2] recognizes an abnormal reaction to alcohol. They describe *Alcohol Idiosyncratic Intoxication* as:

"Maladaptive behavioral changes, e.g., aggressive or assaultive behavior, occurring within minutes of ingesting an amount of alcohol insufficient to induce intoxication in most people. The behavior is atypical of the person when not drinking. . . . Prevalence: Apparently uncommon."

Uncommon? Again, I wonder. Their description of Idiosyncratic Intoxication sounds like the drinking history of some of the alcoholics I know. Might not the "war stories" heard in A.A. be variations on this theme of an abnormal reaction to alcohol?

While it seems obvious that alcoholics drink for psychological reasons, being obvious doesn't make something true. Otherwise the world would be flat, and the Sun would revolve around the Earth.

I think alcoholics drink for all the same reasons anyone else drinks; to relax, for instance. But that alone isn't alcoholism. That isn't what *makes* alcoholics drink. Alcoholics drink because they have to, because they react differently to alcohol. Alcohol doesn't quench an alcoholic's thirst; it makes them thirsty, and they end up drinking too much, one more time. [3]

The Opposing View

Psychiatry is a branch of medicine and professionals in the field of medicine generally accept the psychiatric opinion that alcoholism is a symptom of an underlying psychiatric problem. Tell a physician you're an alcoholic and, rather than withholding tranquilizers as he should, he may interpret your statement to mean that you have a sensitive nature and need more sedation than the average patient.

Doctors prescribe pills all day long. Why should they consider a self-proclaimed alcoholic any different from any other patient aside from the fact that alcoholics are, to the doctor's way of thinking, *addiction prone*, or have a so-called *alcoholic personality* or a *chemical imbalance?*

Psychiatrists specialize in talking, in listening, and in psychopharmacology (psycho-farm-a-col-o-gee), the use of mind-affecting prescription drugs to treat mental and emotional illnesses. Even when doing psychotherapy, they commonly prescribe drugs to help patients relax and feel better while talking. Indeed, some psychiatrists write more prescriptions than physicians in any other branch of medicine.

> *It doesn't usually occur to physicians to change their prescribing habits when prescribing for an alcoholic. They don't ordinarily think of alcoholics as reacting differently to drugs than do nonalcoholics.*

In the minds of most psychiatrists and perhaps most physicians, alcoholism is still a psychiatric symptom, a symptom that demands treatment with mind-affecting drugs. However, because these drugs act on the brain in a manner similar to alcohol, alcoholics often react abnormally to them. They become dependent on the drug, or they return to drinking, or they become dependent on the drug and return to drinking. These medications should be prescribed for recovering alcoholics only after considerable hesitation, and

_____

only in the absence of adequate nonchemical
alternatives.

Even when doctors are concerned about
prescribing an addicting medication to an
alcoholic, they believe they can prevent addiction
by monitoring the number of prescription refills.
They think they can prevent addiction by refusing
further refills after they notice that the patient is
"abusing" the medication.

Abuse, to a doctor, means taking more pills than
prescribed. The cause of abuse is thought to reside
in the so-called addiction-prone patient, not in the
pill. The idea of the patient being the victim of an
abnormal response to the pill (as he or she is to
alcohol) is seldom considered. Nor is it generally
recognized that by the time the patient is found
to be abusing the pills, the disease is already active
and needs treatment, not prevention.

How This Affects You

The topic of prescription pills provokes
controversy among alcoholics. Those who
should continue their medications often look for
excuses to stop. Others use the discussion to
rationalize their continued use.

Those who need an antipsychotic medication such as Haldol, Stelazine or Mellaril are far better off staying sober on the medication than they would be by refusing to take it, losing contact with reality and getting drunk. Likewise, suicidally depressed alcoholics are better off staying sober on an antidepressant than stopping drinking by killing themselves. Furthermore, manic-depressive alcoholics staying sober on lithium are preferable to those who get drunk at the top of the highs or the bottom of the lows of true manic-depressive illness.

Most situations are not this clear-cut. While a disaster may result if an alcoholic ill-advisedly discontinues a needed medication, many recoveries are spoiled by the use of seemingly innocent prescription medications.

If you've ever wondered if you have a pill problem, the following questions might help you decide:

   1. Has your doctor, spouse, or anyone else expressed concern about your use of medications?

   2. Have you ever decided to stop taking pills only to find yourself taking them again contrary to your earlier decision?

3. Have you ever felt remorse or concern about taking pills?

4. Has your efficiency or ambition decreased since taking pills?

5. Have you established a supply for purse or pocket or to hide away in case of emergency?

6. Have you ever been treated by a physician or hospital for excessive use of pills or alcohol?

7. Have you changed doctors or drug stores for the purpose of maintaining your supply?

8. Have you received the same pill from two or more physicians or druggists at approximately the same time?

9. Have you ever been turned down for a refill?

10. Have you taken the same mind- or mood-affecting medication for over a year only to find you still have the same symptoms?

11. Have you ever informed your physician as to which pill works best at which dosage and had him adjust the prescription to your recommendations?

12. Have you used a tranquilizer or a sleep medication for a period of months or years with no improvement in the problem?

13. Have you increased the dosage, strength or frequency of your medication over the past months or years?

14. Is your medication quite important to you; e.g., do you worry about refills long before running out?

15. Do you become annoyed or un-comfortable when others talk about your use of medications?

16. Have you or anyone else noticed a change of personality when you take your medication?

17. Have you ever taken your medication before you had the associated symptom?

18. Have you ever been embarrassed by your behavior when under the influence of your prescription drug?

19. Do you ever sneak or hide your pills?

20. Do you find it impossible to stop or to go for a prolonged period without your pills?

If you've answered "Yes" to a number of these questions, you might want to discuss this matter with your Sponsor and with A.A. members who have had experience with prescription pill addiction.

_____

Not all mind- or mood-affecting medications are equally dangerous for recovering alcoholics. Listed below are several categories of medications with brief comments regarding the relative dangers of each.

Minor Tranquilizers

Trade names include Librium, Valium, Ativan, Tranxene, Xanax and many others. Don't be deceived by the word "minor". "Minor" refers to the fact that these drugs are effective in treating relatively minor psychiatric symptoms such as simple nervousness, agitation or alcohol withdrawal. Alcohol is a minor tranquilizer, and taking any of these drugs can have an effect similar to drinking alcohol.

The symptoms of addiction to these drugs are remarkably similar to those of addiction to alcohol. However, they appear later, persist longer and are more difficult to overcome. For this reason, patients addicted to both alcohol and prescription pills may go through a "double withdrawal," first from alcohol and then from tranquilizers.

Major Tranquilizers

Trade names include Thorazine, Stelazene, Haldol, Mellaril and many others. These drugs are useful in treating psychoses, major psychiatric conditions such as schizophrenia, paranoia and the hallucinations of delirium tremens. Because they are less addicting and the conditions for which they are prescribed are more serious, patients should rely on their physician's advice regarding their use.

Antidepressants

Examples include Asendin, Desyrel, Elavil, Ludiomil, Tofranil and more recently, Prozac, Zoloft, Paxil, Effexor and related chemicals. At present, these drugs don't appear to be addicting and they are often quite beneficial in *true* depression. On the other hand, it doesn't make sense to medicate the depression of early recovery and the minor bouts of depression which are a part of everyday life. These get better on their own without medical intervention.

Likewise, a few years into recovery, some alcoholics develop the "blahs," a sort of "Is that all there is?" feeling. They wonder if maybe they're in a depression and should see a therapist, or they

---

think maybe they need a medication, or maybe they have some sort of chemical imbalance.

Many times, dramatic improvement in this condition follows a redoing of each of the Twelve Steps. Especially when the negative feelings are treated as a defect of character in the Sixth and Seventh Steps.

Regarding Prozac, you can learn more than you need to know about its beneficial effects by reading Kramer's highly advertised *Listening To Prozac*. [4] To learn about its dangers, read *Talking Back To Prozac* [5] by Breggin who also wrote *Toxic Psychaitry*. [6]

Sleeping Pills

Examples include Halcion, Dalmane, Restoril, Noludar, Nembutal and Seconal. These medications are as dangerous or more dangerous than the minor tranquilizers. Alcoholics who use them put their sobriety at considerable risk. The risk extends to the use of nonprescription medications such as Sominex, asking a physician for "something mild" or considering a pill safe simply because it is "new." These are merely ways of continuing to seek chemical answers to life's living problems, and sleep is, for many of us, one of life's living problems. Temporary difficulties in sleeping are common after years of dependence on the sedative drug, alcohol. Unmedicated, the sleep pattern returns to normal. [7]

Cough Preparations

When you pick up a bottle of cough syrup, read the label. According to law, if it contains alcohol, the label will state the amount. In sharp contrast, until recently, the law forbad the listing of the alcohol content on a bottle of beer. Some cough preparations contain codeine. Others contain antihistamines which can have a sedative effect and cause sleepiness.

Ornacol capsules contain no alcohol, codeine, or antihistamines and are available without a prescription. Alcohol-free, liquid cough preparations not requiring a prescription include Ornacol syrup and syrup of Triaminicol. Your pharmacist can recommend many others. And doctors will prescribe an alcohol-free cough preparation if requested. Syrup of Hycomine or Hycodan, Tussionex Suspension and Actifed-C Expectorant are examples.

Emergencies & Postoperative Pain

When the medical situation demands their use, recovering alcoholic patients can safely take sedative and pain-relieving medications such as Demerol and morphine in their customary dosages. However, these drugs should be discontinued as soon as practical. The longer they are continued, the more likely the alcoholic is to get into trouble.

Obviously, recovering alcoholics who are taking narcotic drugs for whatever reason should intensify their recovery program. They can do this, for example, by increasing the number of A.A. meetings they attend, by encouraging visits by A.A. members, by openly discussing their fears and their use of medications, by frequent reading of the Big Book and by listening to audiotapes of A.A. meetings.

Pain Medications

Aspirin, Tylenol, Advil, Motrin and all the non-steroidal anti-inflammatory agents used for arthritic and similar pain are nonaddicting and are in that sense safe for alcoholics. Darvon and codeine are different in that alcoholics do become addicted to them.

Don't concern yourself about Novocaine or other local anesthetics used by your dentist while in his or her office. However, be careful when leaving. Dentists often send patients home with a fairly large supply of codeine or Vicodin.

For chronic pain become familiar with the many effective, non-chemical methods of treating pain. A good place to start would be Dr. Norman J. Marcus' new book *Freedom From Chronic Pain* [8] or Charles Stacy's *The Fight Against Pain.* [9] If you prefer a video, start with Bill Moyers' video series *Healing And The Mind.* [10]

Pep Pills

Pep pills and appetite suppressants such as Dexamyl, Desoxyn, Ionamin, Pondimin and all the amphetamines are quite addictive and should be avoided by all alcoholics (and nonalcoholics).

Anticonvulsants

Examples include Dilantin, Mysoline and Tegretol. They are nonaddicting and affect alcoholics no differently than nonalcoholics. Even the phenobarbital in Dilantin with phenobarbital doesn't seem to cause significant trouble.

Lithium

L ithium is singularly effective in helping to control the excessive mood swings of manic-depressive illness. It particularly suppresses the upward swings, the ones that make the patient feel so good. Perhaps for this reason, patients often stop taking their lithium.

Lithium has a variety of important side-effects when not taken exactly as prescribed. The exact dosage depends on periodic blood tests to determine the blood level of the drug.

When doctors first discovered the effect of lithium on manic-depressive illness, they expressed considerable surprise and jubilation, and they predicted that it would soon become the drug of choice in the treatment of alcoholism. Such has not been the case. Not every alcoholic showing swings of mood has manic-depressive illness. Besides, in time, the serenity of a good recovery program tends to smooth out many of these emotional ups and downs.

Newer Antidepressants and Tranquilizers

A lthough I have had no direct clinical experience with these newer anti-depressants and tranquilizers, I understand they can be quite effective in the treatment of true depression. As to whether or not they are habit-forming or have other undesirable long-term side effects, medications routinely enter the market with a good record in this regard. Reports of these problems don't appear until much later, not until after patients have become addicted and developed long-term side effects, and alcoholics have gotten drunk.

Patients recovering from alcohol or other chemical dependencies face an additional risk when their doctor prescribes a medication to control their emotions. By doing this, the doctor implicitly gives credibility to one of the patient's most troublesome beliefs: The belief that, if things get bad enough, a person can always turn to a chemical answer to life's problems. Over time, the patient relies more and more on the doctor and the pill than on their personal recovery program. The distinction between tranquillity and serenity becomes blurred. Tranquillity of this sort always comes in a bottle and is never more than a cheap imitation of serenity.

What I Wish Doctors Believed

Alcoholics and other chemically-dependent patients would have fewer problems with prescription drugs if all doctors believed as I do.

An alcoholic can't consistently stop drinking after the first drink, and can't, on his own, comfortably and permanently abstain from drinking. That, I believe, is the disease, alcoholism.

As I see it, the underlying cause of alcoholism is an alteration in the chemistry of the brain in a susceptible individual. Just as a patient allergic to penicillin cannot safely use antibiotics of the penicillin type, and a patient allergic to aspirin cannot safely use aspirin-like pain medications, so too a patient allergic to alcohol cannot safely use many of the common mood-affecting medications.

Furthermore, this abnormal response to alcohol and to mood-affecting medications is shared by patients with a history of addiction to cocaine, narcotics, prescription pills and other chemicals. Like alcoholics, their recovery depends on total, permanent abstinence from alcohol and mood-affecting chemicals. And, like alcoholics, their continuing recovery depends on involvement with others with the same problem in a mutual recovery program such as Alcoholics Anonymous, Cocaine Anonymous, Narcotics Anonymous, Pills Anonymous or other Anonymous programs.

I believe physicians can be of service to their alcoholic, pill-addicted and other-addicted patients by establishing the diagnosis, or by accepting the diagnosis when it has already been accepted by the patient. He can help further by encouraging lifelong association with an appropriate recovery group and by consistently refusing to prescribe chemicals conducive to a return to drinking or to the "abuse" of medications.

What To Tell Your Physician

When alcoholics get into trouble as a result of taking prescription pills, they often complain, "I told him I was an alcoholic, and he gave them to me anyway." The problem, as mentioned earlier, is that doctors don't always understand what we mean when we say we are "alcoholic." Here is an example of wording a doctor would probably understand:

> "I am recovering from alcoholism (chemical dependency) and am anxious to refrain from the use of prescription medications which might result in a relapse. I understand the dangerous drugs to be those that affect the mind or mood, such as minor tranquilizers, sedatives, sleeping pills, amphetamines, and narcotics.
>
> "Please consider me sensitive or allergic or as reacting abnormally to these drugs and note this in my chart. I wish to openly discuss with you any situation which you believe calls for their use.

"Thank you sincerely for your cooperation in this matter and for your ongoing concern for my welfare."

Conclusion

As practicing alcoholics, we couldn't control how much we drank once we started, and we couldn't keep from starting. In sobriety, with the help of a Higher Power and the Steps of A.A., we transcend that problem.

This same combination of Steps and Higher Power allows us to live comfortably with the fact that sometimes we must take a prescribed medication. It also gives us a plan of action whereby we avoid the use of medications to control our emotions.

In both situations, acceptance is the answer. We have learned to depend on spiritual rather than chemical answers to our living problems. Ultimately, we are grateful to not have to rely on alcohol and pills as do so many people who lack a Higher Power and a Twelve Step program.

References:

1. Goodman and Gilman's *The Pharmacological Basis of Therapeutics*, 7th ed. (New York: Macmillan Publishing Company, 1985).

2. American Psychiatric Association, *Diagnostic and Statistical Manual of Mental Disorders*, 3rd ed., Revised, (Washington, DC: American Psychiatric Association, 1987).

3. See Chapter 1, *Physical Sobriety*.

4. Peter D. Kramer, *Listening To Prozac*, (New York: Penguin Books, 1994).

5. Peter R. Breggin, *Talking Back To Prozac*, (New York: St. Martin's Press, 1994).

6. Peter R. Breggin, *Toxic Psychiatry*, (New York: St. Martin's Press, 1991).

7. See Addendum B, *Sleeping Without Pills*.

8. Norman J. Marcus and Jean S. Arbeiter, *Freedom From Chronic Pain*, (New York City: Simon & Schuster, 1994).

9. Charles B. Stacy, Andew S. Kaplan and Gray Williams, *The Fight Against Pain*, (Yonkers, New York: Consumer Reports Books, A Division of Consumers Union, 1992).

10. Bill Moyers, *Healing And The Mind*, (New York City: Ambrose Video Publishing, Inc., 1993).

*For a good night's sleep, I had to give up my old
ideas about sleep.*

SLEEPING WITHOUT PILLS
Sleeping

Insomnia

Insomniacs recovering from alcoholism are lucky. They already know from personal experience that recovery from alcoholism depends on willingness to surrender. In like manner, recovery from insomnia is another example of surrendering to win.

In A.A., by surrendering to our powerlessness, we transcend our drinking problem. Then, those of us who suffer from insomnia discover that the power that keeps us sober during the day also works at night.

Alcoholics have sleep problems because alcohol and sleeping pills suppress the REM (Rapid Eye Movement) sleep pattern. This doesn't return to normal immediately in sobriety. Indeed, it may never do so if periodically disturbed by the use of alcohol or sleep medications. Newcomers in recovery are well advised to have a medical checkup but to decline offers of prescriptions for sleeping pills.

Living consists of problems, and, for many of us, sleeping is one of those problems. Our first inclination is to "take something" to help us sleep. We are headed for trouble if we do because that intensifies the problem. The better the chemical works, the less likely we are to sleep well thereafter without it. With continued use, more of the chemical is required to get the same effect, and the effect lasts for progressively shorter periods of time. Eventually, other chemicals must be added to counteract the side-effects which develop from the excessive use of the first chemical.

Working On The Problem

Insomnia is a nuisance, not a disease. It should not be medicated. Besides, few things stimulate insomnia more than a decision to "work" on it. Insomnia always accepts the challenge.

I must have been born with insomnia. I fought it all through my pre-A.A. life and early sobriety. In the late 1930's while attending pharmacy school, I discovered what I thought would be the answer to my sleep problem. After putting in a hard day's work at school, working in the family drug store all evening and then studying into the wee hours of the night, I found that a couple beers allowed me to jump in bed, sleep real fast and wake up smart. Better living through chemistry soon became my way of life.

For the next thirty years I literally worked on the problem of relaxing. I did everything I could think of and took every drug I could find that might force me to sleep. The harder I worked on the problem, the worse it got; and the worse it got, the harder I worked on it. Toward the end, in addition to alcohol and pills, it took two intravenous injections of barbiturates administered surreptitiously in the garage to get me through the night. Even so, it wasn't a particularly restful sleep. Certainly what I was doing couldn't be described as "social sleeping."

Today I realize that I thought of sleep as a period of unconsciousness preceded by a period of increasing drowsiness. Furthermore, I had been misinformed that everyone needed at least eight hours sleep every night, and I set out to get my full quota.

New Ideas

The military services have conducted experiments to determine the minimum requirements for sleep and the maximum length of time a man can be forcibly kept awake. These studies have shown that, while periods of relaxation are indeed quite important, a total lack of consciousness is not necessary. On the other hand, even using strong persuasion, it is impossible to keep the mind awake once it decides to go to sleep. The mind will sleep, even if for only brief periods of time, no matter what one does to keep it awake.

These brief mini-sleeps are of extreme importance to those of us with sleep problems. They form the basis for the statement that "no one ever died from lack of sleep." They also explain why it is impossible to commit suicide by staying awake, as opposed to taking an overdose of pills and sleeping oneself to death.

Even those who can sleep any time they want can't really control their state of consciousness. They can't lose and regain consciousness at will. They can do things conducive to losing consciousness or waking up, but they can't literally *make* it happen.

Unconsciousness. Therein lies the answer to our sleep problem. We must stop demanding unconsciousness. We must stop trying to manage something over which we are powerless.

Our only recourse is to relax, stop struggling and let go. We must learn to turn over to the care of God, not only our will and our lives, but also our sleep. After we do that, how much sleep we get is no longer our concern. It's His. And if we should die from lack of sleep, it's His fault.

Turning over a sleep problem to God is like turning over any other problem. If we continue to have any idea as to how He ought to handle it, we haven't really turned it over.

Surrender comes first (giving up all opinions, notions and beliefs as to our nocturnal needs and wants), then relaxation, then acceptance — grateful acceptance of whatever God sends us throughout the night.

How To Sleep Without Pills

Because I haven't yet perfected any part of my recovery program, I still sleep poorly at times. When this happens, I don't talk about it or allow it to affect my mood or activities the next day. When I tell someone I am tired, I give them a totally useless piece of information. They can't help me. And even more important, I admit to them and to myself that a simple sleep problem has the power to control my day and my life. Then, to regain control of my life, I insist on more sleep, and I attempt to get it by trying to control something over which I am powerless.

Worrying about whether or not I get enough sleep is an old way of thinking which I have had to give up. The title of one of Terry Cole-Whittaker's books is "What You Think of Me is None of My Business." [1] I prefer to think of it as, "Whether or Not I Get Enough Sleep is None of My Business."

On the other hand, we can't ask God to help us sleep if we don't cooperate. Many alcoholics complain of restless nights while they continue to smoke cigarettes and drink beverages loaded with caffeine and sugar. This doesn't matter, they insist, because they have no trouble getting to sleep; their problem is staying asleep. My experience tells me we sleep better after we give ourselves four to six or more weeks without caffeine and excessive sugar, and preferably also without nicotine or chocolate.

One of many techniques for relaxing to get to sleep is known as progressive muscle relaxation. To practice it, lie quietly and make a tight fist to see how contracted muscles feel, then relax your fist to see how relaxation feels. Repeat this procedure until you are familiar with the feeling of relaxation. Now, eliminate the contraction phase and relax the toes on one foot, then on the other. Next one foot and ankle, then the other. Then each calf and each thigh. Slowly progress upward through all the muscles of the body including the face and scalp. Repeat this relaxing procedure until sleep intervenes.

A similar method focuses attention on the joints rather than the muscles. Lie very still. Focus your attention on first one toe and then another. Ask yourself the exact location of each toe in relation to the other toes and the rest of my body. Do not move the toe to answer the question. Is it bent or straight? What is it touching? After carefully and thoroughly checking each toe, check one ankle joint, then the other, then the knees, the hips, the spine and eventually every joint in the body.

If still awake, count backwards from five hundred by 3's. Allow yourself to think of nothing else and start over every time you get lost or begin to fall asleep. If you dislike arithmetic as much as I do, your mind will rebel and shut itself off.

On other occasions you can count backwards from
five hundred by 1's, carefully visualizing every
number: 4-9-9, 4-9-8, 4-9-7, 4-9-6, etc.

As I see it, the trick for me in all these techniques
is to assume the role of choirmaster and get all
the voices in my head to focus on one, single, bland
sentence or thought. In time, the voices quiet down
and disappear. I open my eyes and find it's
suddenly much later than it was. Or, to state it
differently, while thinking a thought, I lose
consciousness and wake up thinking the same
thought without realizing I've been asleep.

These mini-sleeps are extremely important
because they add up during the night when I lie
quietly and allow them to happen. But, while
anticipating and doing everything I can to
encourage them, I dare not try to *make* them
happen.

Although these minisleeps recur again and again
and again, I'm still pleasantly surprised and
grateful every time they happen.

During the night, I never check on the time.
Lacking any middle-of-the-night appointments,
my only reason for watching the time would be to
decide how tired to be the next day. Merely
glancing at the clock aggravates my problem by

taking my mind off the answer and refocusing it on the problem.

Add The Program

The techniques mentioned so far can be used by nonalcoholics as well as alcoholics. But for me the real answers to a sleep problem come from the A.A. program. If I keep the Big Book at my bedside and read when I can't sleep, I can't lose. I'll either become an expert on the Big Book, or on sleeping, or on both. I find particularly appropriate the Book's strong admonition, expressed twice, that we cease fighting anything or anybody. [2] I understand this to include fighting sleep and the nocturnal voices in my head.

During the day, I often relax, close my eyes and enjoy a short, refreshing catnap. At night, I read until I find myself re-reading the same paragraphs. After turning out the light, I keep my mind focused on a single, simple thought such as, *If God be with me, who can be against me?* Or I recite and meditate on the meaning of the Serenity Prayer or the Third Step Prayer or the Seventh Step Prayer. At other times I recite and dwell on the precise meaning of the Twelve Steps. Formerly, when all else failed, I played an A.A. tape.

Currently my sleep program consists of:

1. Allowing my muscles and joints to relax.

2. Being completely satisfied with and optimistic about mini-sleeps with *no* demands for drowsiness.

3. Breathing diaphragmatically (also known as abdominally). The abdomen (belly) swells with each inhalation and contracts with each exhalation. The incoming air flows *downward* rather than *upward*. (This is an excellent way to breathe when tense or nervous, or when about to speak in public, or at any time.)

4. Allowing my mind to think about *nothing* but how I am breathing and the very important fact that God resides deep within me.

5. *Persisting* in this program even when it seems obvious that it isn't working.

As a result of this program, most of my nights are now both physically relaxing and spiritually stimulating.

Conclusion

Faced with the problem of alcoholism, I fought it as long and as hard as I could. When I could fight no longer, I surrendered and gave the problem to my Higher Power. At that point, I won. I became comfortable. The problem ceased to be a problem, and I am now spiritually and emotionally stronger for having surrendered to my drinking problem.

My sleep problem shares a similar history. I had to let go of it. I had to give it to my Higher Power. Then I had to pray, not for sleep, but for the willingness to lie awake waiting for Him to decide whether or not I lost consciousness.

This combination of willingness to lie awake and be satisfied with mini-sleeps, plus focused, single-thought thinking, provides me with all the sleep I need. [3] And, in addition, as with my alcoholism, I am a spiritually and emotionally stronger person for having had the problem and for having surrendered to it.

References:

1. Terry Cole-Whittaker, *What You Think Of Me Is None Of My Business*, (Stamford, CT: Oak Tree Pulications, Inc., 1979).

2. *Alcoholics Anonymous*, 3rd ed. (New York City: Alcoholics Anonymous World Services, Inc., 1976), pp. 84 & 103

3. For a more detailed discussion of the power of thinking, see Chapter 2, *Mental Sobriety*.

Afterword

Well, it's been a long journey. The manuscript is finished and the pages are formatted and ready for printing. They'll soon be bound and turned into a book. I have a sense of accomplishment at having brought the project this far.

I've often wondered if putting this book together has been an ego trip for me. But every time I decided to give it up, friends have urged me to keep going. Furthermore, I have repeatedly recited a modified version of the third step prayer in which I offer myself *and* the manuscript to God to do with as He wishes. It has been and it continues to be entirely up to Him as to what happens next.

I've benefitted a great deal from writing this, and I hope someone benefits from reading it. And if a profit should develop from the sale of it, the Mary Lind Foundation (recovery homes for alcoholics) will certainly benefit from that.

"Not only has Dr. Paul targeted problems that face most of us today, he offers invaluable resources and applicable solutions coupled with a light touch and his enjoyable wit. He has a spiritual and humble nature which is woven throughout this book. He incorporates answers for even those questions we hadn't yet realized we needed to ask." — *Sue M., M.F.C.C., Private Practice.*

"Here is a road map of recovery, written in a bright, witty style, which describes ways to cut through a lifetime of mental red tape. Do you want a life of resignation, or do you want a spiritual life that is refreshing and rejuvenated? The choice is yours. This book presents a practical guide for ways of nourishing and enriching your spiritual, mental, physical and social journey through 'The Land Of Beginning Again.' " —*Ruthanne S., Ph.D., Human Services Counseling Clinic, Supervisor.*

"What fun! This book is delightful and a great example of *Rule 62.*[1] I really support your publishing this and making it available. It's a joy to read and *filled* with useful and helpful information. The parts which deal with neurochemistry are accurate and totally in line with what I believe. As we change our behavior through the steps and the program, our thinking (our brain chemistry) is restored to sanity, is restored to clarity." — *Scott B., Ph.D., Professor at a prominent University Medical School.*

1. "Don't take yourself too damn seriously," *The Twelve Steps and Twelve Traditions,* (New York City: Alcoholics Anonymous World Services, Inc., 1953), Tradition Four, p. 153 (with permission).

Share this book with your friends

Purchase Information

There's More To Quitting Drinking Than Quitting Drinking by Dr.Paul O.

$14.95 per copy

$3.00 Postage & Handling for first copy (US only)
$0.50 each additional copy
$1.16 Sales Tax each copy (CA residents only)
Quantity discounts available to book sellers & treatment centers
(1998 prices subject to change without notice)

(<u>Also</u> available as a **Talking Book** read by Fr. Tom W.)
(Four cassettes...$31.75+tax Call 1-800-537-6767)

Master or Visa credit card, check or money order

SOUTH BAY BOOKS
P.O. Box 3272
Torrance, CA 90510-3272
1-888-5BOOKS5
1-888-526-6575
Fax 1-310-326-4417
www.southbaybooks.com

or

ISLEWEST PUBLISHING
4242 Chavanelle Road
Dubuque, IA 52002-2650
1-800-557-9867
Fax 1-319-557-1376
e-mail: mjgraham@carcomm.com

Sabrina Publishing
P.O. Box 6722
Laguna Niguel, CA 92607-6722